Changes in Income Inequality within U.S. Metropolitan Areas

Janice F. Madden

2000

W.E. Upjohn Institute for Employment Research
Kalamazoo, Michigan

Library of Congress Cataloging-in-Publication Data

Madden, Janice Fanning.
    Changes in income inequality within U.S. metropolitan areas / Janice F. Madden.
      p. cm.
    Includes bibliographical references and index.
    ISBN 0–88099–204–2 (alk. paper). — ISBN 0–88099–203–4 (pbk. : alk. paper)
      1. Income distribution—United States. I. Title.
HC110.I5 M23 2000
339.2'2'0973091724—dc21

00–023017

The facts presented in this study and the observations and viewpoints expressed are the sole responsibility of the author. They do not necessarily represent positions of the W.E. Upjohn Institute for Employment Research.

Cover design by J.R. Underhill.
Index prepared by Diane Worden.
Printed in the United States of America.

To my children,

Patrick and Erin

Contents

List of Figures

List of Tables

Preface

Ten years ago, as co-Director of the Temple-Penn Philadelphia Economic Monitoring Project, I was surprised to find that Philadelphia had not experienced as much growth in income inequality during the 1980s as the rest of the nation (Madden and Stull 1991). The transition of the Philadelphia economy from manufacturing to producer services spawned an increase in employment in service industries that provided jobs for those who had not been employed, including African-American men and women of all races. As many of these jobs offered relatively low wages, the earnings distribution became more unequal. Because these lower wage workers disproportionately resided in households with incomes at the lower end of the distribution, the post-industrialization of Philadelphia employment appeared to reduce poverty rates. In addition, another demographic factor, a slight decrease in the proportion of households headed by women, also operated to decrease the proportion of Philadelphia households in a demographic group that experienced a high risk of poverty.

These findings for Philadelphia led me to ask whether there were similar relationships between metropolitan characteristics and household income distribution in other metropolitan areas. Metropolitan areas, whose boundaries define unique local labor markets, provide a database for testing the connections between labor market characteristics, demographic compositions, poverty rates and income distributions. This book, the culmination of my investigation of these relationships in 182 U.S. metropolitan areas, provides evidence that the Philadelphia experience can be generalized. While the earnings distribution is an important component of household income inequality and poverty rates, household formation patterns are also critical components. The growth of low wage jobs in the service sector, even with declines in higher wage jobs in manufacturing, reduces poverty and income inequality if the new service sector jobs go to those who previously had no jobs.

Several research assistants were involved in the project, and I am grateful to all of them. Early on, Andrew Haughwout used the Current Population Survey data to compute Gini coefficients for several large metropolitan areas and demonstrate that there were interesting differences across areas; he also shared with me his data on changes in the physical size of cities in the 1980s. Pierre Vilain wrote the programs that computed the various Gini coefficients and the quintile shares for the 182 metropolitan areas in this study, using the 1980 and 1990 Public Use Micro Samples. Rosa Gross reviewed maps and documentation on changes in metropolitan area boundaries between the 1980 and 1990 Census. Carlos Grushka assisted in running several of the regression analyses. Kate Offutt provided final checks on the data reported here; she re-ran all of the analyses included in this text.

Several colleagues provided comments and suggestions on various parts of this work. Participants in the Penn Population Studies Colloquium, the Penn Department of Real Estate Seminar, the Society of Labor Economics meeting, and the North American Regional Science Association meeting provided useful comments on presentations of this work. I am particularly grateful to Joseph Gyourko, Jerry Jacobs, Janet Pack, and Anita Summers for their comments. Special thanks are due to Timothy Bartik for his faith in this project and his numerous suggestions of ways to improve it. David Nadziejka provided careful and patient editorial assistance.

My research was funded by the University of Pennsylvania, the Department of Real Estate at the Wharton School, the National Science Foundation (SBR-9348793), and the W.E. Upjohn Foundation for Employment Research.

The Author

Janice F. Madden is the Robert C. Daniels Term Professor of Urban Studies, Regional Science, Sociology, and Real Estate at the University of Pennsylvania. She served as Vice Provost for Graduate Education from 1991 to 1999. Prof. Madden came to Penn in 1972 after completing her graduate studies in economics at Duke University. She joined the demography group in the Department of Sociology in 1994, and she served as Director of the Women's Studies Program from 1988 to 1991. Her research dealing with the effects of race, gender, and urban location on labor market outcomes and metropolitan variations in income distribution has been published in a variety of journals. She has written three other books: *The Economics of Sex Discrimination* (1972); *Post-Industrial Philadelphia* (1990); and *Work, Wages, and Poverty* (1991).

1 Income Inequality, Earnings Inequality, and Poverty

During the 1980s, a wide variety of measures showed trends toward rising economic inequality. Inequality in the distribution of income among households within U.S. metropolitan areas increased by almost 11 percent.[1] The average poverty rate increased by over 9 percent in metropolitan areas and by almost 18 percent in their central cities.[2] These disparities grew while mean real[3] per capita household income increased by 22 percent. The distribution of earnings among workers also diverged; for example, inequality grew by almost 10 percent among male workers.

As disparities grew in income (among households) and in earnings (among workers) as well as between cities and their suburbs throughout the nation, there were also sizeable differences among metropolitan areas. Some experienced only slight increases in the inequality of their income distribution, and a few experienced a slight decrease;[4] but for others, there was substantial growth in inequality.

Figure 1.1 illustrates the change in household income inequality for some U.S. metropolitan statistical areas (MSAs) between 1979 and 1989.[5] Pittsburgh experienced the greatest percentage increase in income inequality, 23 percent; on the other side of the state, Philadelphia experienced a much lower increase of only 4 percent. Of the large MSAs in Figure 1.1, Washington and San Diego had the least growth in household income inequality; Cleveland and Buffalo in the Midwest and New Orleans, Houston, and Miami in the South experienced fairly large increases.

The reasons for the wide variation in MSA income inequality during the 1980s are not clear. Regional location is not obviously associated with the differences. Western MSAs (e.g., Seattle, San Francisco, Los Angeles, and San Diego) are represented in the entire range of experiences, as are Eastern MSAs (e.g., Boston, Baltimore, Philadelphia, and Washington). Large metropolitan areas experienced greater increases in inequality (e.g., Houston) and also lesser increases (e.g., Philadelphia).

1

Figure 1.1 Percentage Change in Household Income Gini Coefficient, 1979–1989

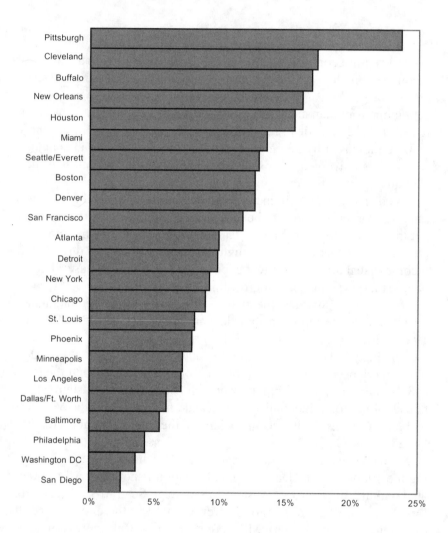

Neither do local labor market conditions provide an obvious explanation. Figure 1.2 shows the percentage change in earnings (wage or salary) inequality among individual workers in the same MSAs for 1979–1989. A comparison of Figures 1.1 and 1.2 yields no obvious pattern. While Pittsburgh had the greatest growth in both income inequality and earnings inequality, there is no pattern for the other MSAs. Dallas experienced a greater increase in earnings inequality than Atlanta, even though Atlanta had a much greater increase in household income inequality. Seattle, Minneapolis, and Baltimore had only a slight growth in earnings inequality. It is not obvious why Los Angeles and Dallas had relatively large increases in earnings inequality while Phoenix, Miami, and Boston experienced lesser increases.

The poverty rate varies among MSAs and also within MSAs, because central city poverty rates exceed the rates in the surrounding suburbs. In 1979, 11.7 percent of persons in the average MSA had incomes below the poverty line; the percentage grew to 12.7 percent in 1989. Poverty rates in the central cities of MSAs were higher, an average of 15.9 percent in 1979 and 18.5 percent in 1989. The highest poverty rate in 1989 for the 182 largest MSAs was in McAllen, Texas, and the highest rate for central cities was in Benton Harbor, Michigan. The lowest poverty rate for an MSA with a central city was for Stamford, Connecticut, at 6.3 percent. Overall, the poverty rates within cities have exceeded both the national rate and the rate for their surrounding suburbs.

Figure 1.3 illustrates the tendency over the last 20 years for poverty to concentrate within the central cities of MSAs. The figure portrays the ratios of central city poverty rates to the overall MSA rates in 1969, 1979, and 1989 for 50 of the largest MSAs. In 1979, central city poverty rates for the 182 largest MSAs averaged 40 percent higher than the rates for their metropolitan areas. The largest difference was in Hartford, where the 1979 central city rate was 319 percent of the metropolitan rate and the lowest was in McAllen, Texas, where the 1979 central city rate was lower than the MSA rate. The difference between the average central city poverty rate and the rate for its MSA grew by 8 percent over the decade 1980–1989, continuing the trend of the prior decade. The increases between 1969 and 1989 appear most dramatic among those MSAs that had the greatest concentration of poverty in the central city in 1969. Philadelphia, Birmingham, San Diego, and

Figure 1.2 Percentage Change in Earnings Gini Coefficient, 1979–1989

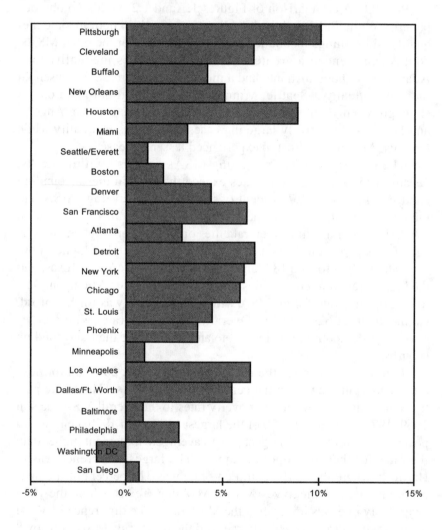

Albany stand out as exceptions, cities with less concentration in 1969 that grew more dramatically in concentration.

There is no pattern that links the MSAs and central cities having the most or the least poverty to those having the most even or the most uneven income distributions. We do not understand why poverty rates, household income inequality, and earnings inequality vary across these local economies. Although there has been little investigation of differences in the rates of change in income inequality across U.S. MSAs, there has been extensive research on rising income inequality within the nation as a whole. It is now widely accepted both that the distributions of income across households and of wages/salaries across workers (Levy and Murnane 1992) have become more unequal in the 1980s, and that the differences in income and several other social and economic characteristics between suburban and city residents have increased (Reich 1991; Getis 1988; Cutler and Glaeser 1995; Massey 1999).

Knowledge of the circumstances surrounding changes in metropolitan income inequality is essential to our understanding of how the larger economy (the "macro-environment" of the marketplace) affects income distributions. We cannot respond with economic or social policies (or even decide not to respond) to changes in income inequality and other metropolitan economic issues without such knowledge. To show why this is so, it is helpful to briefly review the reasons policymakers and scholars are concerned with inequality in the first place. Those reasons clarify why household income inequality in particular is of concern and why a metropolitan area is an appropriate unit to use when measuring such inequality as an outcome of the economy or marketplace.

WHY IS INEQUALITY OF CONCERN?

The concerns about rising inequality arise from fundamental notions of fairness and social justice based on philosophical premises, on the desires of the electorate, or on more pragmatic concerns. The most influential scholarship that develops criteria for evaluating alternative distributions is John Rawls' (1971) landmark book, *A Theory of*

Figure 1.3 Ratio of Central City to MSA Poverty, 1969–1989

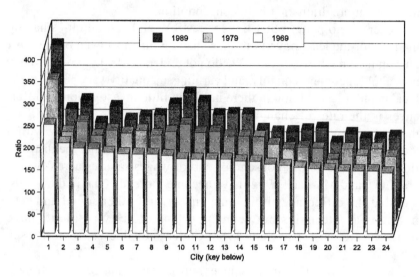

Key

1	Hartford	13	Cincinnati
2	Washington	14	Baltimore
3	Cleveland	15	Pittsburgh
4	Boston	16	Chicago
5	Providence	17	Louisville
6	Minneapolis	18	Salt Lake City
7	St. Louis	19	Milwaukee
8	Dayton	20	Miami
9	Detroit	21	Denver
10	Atlanta	22	Orlando
11	Rochester	23	San Francisco
12	Buffalo	24	Seattle

Figure 1.3 (continued)

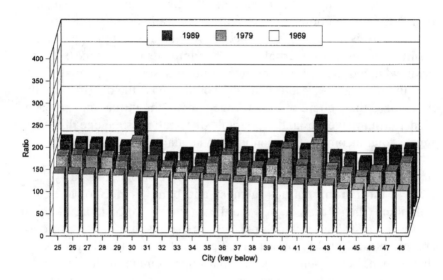

Key

25 Kansas City	37 Charlotte
26 Portland	38 Oklahoma City
27 New Orleans	39 Houston
28 Columbus	40 San Diego
29 Tampa	41 Indianapolis
30 Philadelphia	42 Albany
31 Sacramento	43 San Antonio
32 New York City	44 Jacksonville
33 Los Angeles	45 Phoenix
34 Norfolk	46 Nashville
35 Dallas	47 Memphis
36 Birmingham	48 Greensboro

Justice. Rawls proposed that a desirable or fair distribution is one that the average citizen would prefer over all others if his or her own position in the distribution were not known (i.e., an "original position" in which there is a "veil of ignorance"). Rawls argued that the original position represents impartial and fair judgments of outcomes. Rawls acknowledged that, in the absence of other assumptions about a citizen, the rational risk-neutral citizen would choose the distribution that maximizes the welfare of the average person, the utilitarian approach. Under utilitarian criteria, the desirable distribution is the one that maximizes total income in the economy, and equality is not of concern.

For equality to be of concern, one must introduce a concept of justice (or risk aversion). If this same citizen were also motivated by "justice," a motive that values fairness and benevolence toward each individual, then Rawls argued that he or she would be more likely to prefer the distribution which maximizes the absolute welfare or consumption level of the poorest members of the society. Rawls argued that justice, in this sense, implies that improvement of the welfare of society as a whole (as represented by an increase in total income) cannot compensate for the losses experienced by poor members. If citizens are rational, risk-neutral, and motivated by justice, distributions that maximize the well-being of the poorest (i.e., maximin criteria) are preferred. A more unequal distribution is preferred to a more equal one only when it results in additional income for poor individuals. The distribution which yields the greater total income (or average income) is preferred only when sufficient additional income is allocated to the poor to make them absolutely better off than with the more equal distribution. Because "just" social institutions must produce fair outcomes or distributions that maximize the welfare of the poor, Rawls' theory implies that economies having lower poverty rates, or which produce a more equal distribution of the same total income, are more desirable.

If concerns with equality are based on Rawlsian-type principles of fairness and justice, then policymakers seek political/organizational strategies and social institutions that maximize the welfare of the poor in the society. The characteristics of institutions and societies that yield more equal distributions are of central interest to scholars.

The mandate for policymakers to pursue such strategies from the U.S. electorate is less clear. Thurow (1975) argued that income equality is a public policy concern because everyone's well-being is affected by it. Public opinion polls have indicated that although Americans desire more income equality, they are not sufficiently concerned to see governmental intervention, specially federal intervention, as desirable. A 1982 Trendex Inc. poll found that the majority of Americans desired more income equality: 49 percent of Americans thought the difference between the incomes of the rich and the poor was much too great and another 23 percent thought it was somewhat too great (Shapiro, Patterson, and Russell 1987, pp. 126–127). A 1976 Harris Poll showed that only 41 percent of Americans favored using the federal government to make a fairer distribution of wealth in the country (Shapiro, Patterson, and Russell, p. 127). Richard C. Michel (1991) noted that a poll reported in the Washington Post in April of 1990 indicated that only 29 percent of Americans "agreed" or "strongly agreed" that it is the responsibility of government to reduce differences in income. These data contrast with those from other industrialized nations, where the proportions responding that they agreed or strongly agreed with the need for government to reduce differences in income ranged between 60 and 80 percent.

These polls of American opinion do not necessarily conflict with the desirability of egalitarian distributions developed by Rawls. The polls show that Americans favor more equal income distribution, but they lack confidence that government can effectively make income more equal. These results are consistent with a preference for equality that is tempered by fears that government programs to promote greater equality will come at too great a loss in total income.[6]

If concerns with equality are based upon the desires of the American electorate as evidenced in public opinion polls, the implications for both policymakers and scholars are similar to those for concerns with equality based on Rawlsian-type principles of fairness and justice. Given the lack of support for national government intervention but the desire for greater income equality, scholarship that helps to define the characteristics of institutions and societies that yield more equal distributions are of central interest.

Nozick (1974), in a contrary position, contended that income equality is not a government or a public policy concern because government has no income to distribute. Rather, he holds that government defines the rules of operation, and those rules (not the resulting distribution) should be the target of public policy. Even if one grants

Nozick's position, it is difficult to envision how we evaluate or judge "the rules" without reference to their result, the equality of income.

Beyond philosophical ideals, there are more-pragmatic reasons why income inequality is of concern. Rising income inequality undermines political stability (Sommers 1995; Starobin 1995), and some recent studies have indicated that inequality may also lower future economic growth rates (e.g., Benabou 1996; Persson and Tabellini 1994). Such pragmatic reasons for promoting equal distributions lead policymakers and scholars to the search for pragmatic ways of achieving equality: the characteristics of institutions and societies that yield more equal (or less equal) distributions are of central interest.

The concerns about inequality, whether they are based on premises developed by political philosophers, on the desires of the electorate, or on pragmatic concerns with stability or economic growth, are about the well-being (that is, the consumption levels) of individuals. Because the consumption level of individuals depends on the income received by their household, it is the distribution of household income that is the outcome of concern to policymakers and scholars. The distribution of wages or salaries to individual workers is of policy concern only to the extent that it affects consumption or the household income distribution. This issue is discussed in more detail in the next chapter.

WHY ANALYZE METROPOLITAN AREAS?

Policies to encourage greater equality in the distribution of well-being are more than policies to improve the well-being of a set of individuals; they are policies to change the larger (macro) environment in which goods and services are produced and distributed. But, what constitutes the appropriate macro-environment?

There are two considerations in conceptually determining the appropriate dimensions of the macro-environment for which inequality matters. The first is based on information flows and is determined by the physical dimensions of the macro-environment or the distances over which the outcomes (the effects of income differences) are perceived or received by households. The second is based on the dimensions of the environment or unit that produces or transmits the inequality.

Because people are more likely to be aware of how their own income or consumption levels compare with those of fellow MSA residents than with residents of the entire nation, and because well-being is affected (at least in part) by the relationship of one's own consumption to that of one's community, income inequality within the MSA is a more relevant outcome measure for concerns based on fairness and justice or on the electorate's desire for equality. The importance of the characteristics of the MSA to the well-being of residents is reinforced by the tendency of most individuals to stay in the same MSA. While U.S. census data indicate that almost half of Americans residing in metropolitan areas changed their residence between 1985 and 1990, the large majority of these residential moves were within the same MSA. There was much less residential mobility between MSAs: only 16 percent of Americans residing in an MSA in 1990 were living outside that MSA five years earlier. Most Americans stay in the same metropolitan area, even when they change residence and/or job location.[7]

If the social and political cohesiveness of the national electorate is affected by the national distribution of income, the cohesiveness of state and local electorates should be even more susceptible to such influence because the effects of inequality are more immediately obvious.

To the extent that economic or market conditions generate income or wage distributions, metropolitan areas are more "interesting" units than the nation to use in studying inequality. Unlike the nation, or census regions, or states or counties whose boundaries are administratively or politically determined, the definitions of (and the boundaries for) metropolitan areas are based on market or economic criteria. U.S. metropolitan areas are the ideal geographic unit on which to base a subnational analysis of the role of markets, because they are the only subnational areas that represent an economic market. MSA boundaries are drawn based on the degree of economic and social integration of the counties.[8]

The state of Pennsylvania, for example, includes part of the fourth largest metropolitan area in the nation, Philadelphia, but it also includes a large number of rural areas with neither proximity nor strong economic linkages to the Philadelphia economy. Pittsburgh and Erie, metropolitan areas with economies that are more similar in industrial structure and in overall performance to midwestern MSAs such as Cleveland or Indianapolis than they are to Philadelphia, are also included within the Pennsylvania boundaries. Similar descriptions apply to most of the states, especially New York, Georgia, Washington, Texas, Florida, and Illinois.

County boundaries, like state boundaries, are based on political, rather than market, relationships. Furthermore, counties vary widely around the nation, sometimes including several municipalities (such as Allegheny County, which includes the city of Pittsburgh, and Harris County, which includes the city of Houston) and other times being smaller than the city (New York City, which includes Manhattan, Bronx, Brooklyn, Queens, and Staten Island counties, is an obvious example).

It is also problematic to study areas that are smaller than MSAs. Poverty and the distribution of income within cities cannot be analyzed apart from the MSAs in which the cities are located. MSAs constitute the labor market for city and suburban residents. Their very delineation is based on the commuting ranges of workers in the local labor market. Because salaries and wages account for most household income, conditions in the metropolitan labor market, combined with the decisions of individuals to join or leave households and to live in the central city or in the suburbs, influence income distribution and poverty within the central city. Obviously, if municipalities and cities are too small a unit to encompass the relevant labor and housing markets, then smaller units such as census tracts are even more problematic.

In addition to the conceptual reasons for measuring equality within an MSA, the measurement of income inequality within an MSA is more likely to reflect accurately differences in consumption than is inequality measured for the nation. Because the cost of living varies across regions in the United States, differences in income or earnings across the nation do not translate into equivalent differences in consumption when they arise from regional differences in the price of goods and services. Inequality measured within an MSA reflects real differences in consumption because residents of the same MSA have the same cost of living.

THE PLAN OF THE STUDY

This study identifies and quantifies the characteristics of metropolitan economies that are associated with changes in economic inequality in the 1980s. An understanding of how metropolitan characteristics are associated with metropolitan income inequality must underlie any public policy proposals to move toward greater equality of distribution. The uses of such knowledge in guiding policy efforts to alter the trend toward rising inequality are also discussed.

Specifically, the study explores how the demography, the labor market, and the geographic structure of a metropolitan area are related to changes in income inequality.

- Demographics—changes in the age and ethnic composition of the population, as well as changes in the way Americans form families and households—define how income is shared across generations and how earnings and other income flows translate into economic well-being.

- Wages and salaries are the primary source of income for most American households. Changes in the supply of workers, in the demand for workers, and in the way that wages and salaries are determined in the labor market strongly influence the income that flows to U.S. households.

- The neighborhoods and communities where Americans live influence their local tax liabilities, their access to publicly provided goods and services (especially educational opportunities), their personal security and safety, their ability to commute to work, and their understanding and knowledge about occupations, jobs, how to "get things done," etc. Increasing income segmentation and racial segregation of neighborhoods and communities—that is, the locational isolation or concentration of households of different income levels—may affect the growth in inequality in an economy.

Each of these three elements of the macro-environment are "likely suspects" among the factors that could be associated with the increase in income inequality and poverty in U.S. metropolitan areas during the 1980s.

Chapter 2 reviews the explanations for rising inequality that have been proposed for the nation as a whole. I review theories of the role of labor markets, education and skills, economic growth, location, and demographic composition of the population in affecting the extent of inequality.

Chapter 3 introduces data on measures of inequality, poverty, and economic, social, geographic, and demographic characteristics and their changes in U.S. MSAs over the 1980s. The chapter discusses ways that these characteristics of MSAs may be related to one another.

Chapter 4 identifies the problems that must be addressed when studying inequality within U.S. MSAs, including the difficulties inherent in empirically measuring inequality and the determination of the appropriate geographic boundaries of an economic system.

Chapters 5, 6, 7, and 8 report the results of statistical analyses of the relationships between changes between 1979 and 1989 in income inequality, wage inequality, and poverty rates of MSAs, as well as the demographic composition, skill composition, geographic structure, and labor markets. In Chapter 5 household income inequality (as measured by changes in the Gini coefficient of household income) and the shares of income accruing to each quintile of the income distribution are analyzed. Chapter 6 addresses changes in the Gini coefficients for wages and salaries for various groupings of workers and also analyzes the household income Gini coefficient for subgroupings of the population. Chapter 7 addresses changes in the metropolitan poverty rate, and Chapter 8 changes in the concentration of poverty within the central cities of metropolitan areas.

Chapter 9 compiles the results from the analyses of all of the measures of inequality and reviews the public policy implications of the results.

Notes

1. As measured by the mean percentage change in the Gini coefficient for metropolitan household income (see Table 3.1).
2. See Table 3.2.
3. After correcting for the effects of inflation.
4. Stockton, California; Norfolk, Virginia; and Waterbury, Connecticut, were the only metropolitan areas studied here that experienced an increase in household income equality between 1979 and 1989.

5. The measure of inequality is the percentage change between 1979 and 1989 in the Gini coefficient; this coefficient is discussed in greater detail in Chapter 3.

6. These polls are also not polls of Rawls' citizens in the original position, behind "a veil of ignorance." Americans responding to the surveys know where they have ended up in the distribution. Analyses of opinion polls show that social position affects opinions about the desirability of income equality: poorer individuals are more supportive than richer individuals of government efforts at redistribution (Bobo 1991).

7. But, with 16 percent of the typical MSA's population shifting in a five-year period, mobility may change the characteristics of the population of any metropolitan area.

8. MSAs are defined in terms of counties (except for New England, where they are defined in terms of cities and towns). An area is an MSA if it includes either at least one city of at least 50,000 inhabitants or if it includes an urbanized area (as defined by the U.S. Bureau of the Census) of at least 50,000 inhabitants and a total MSA population of at least 100,000. The outlying counties included in an MSA are defined based on their commuting patterns to the central city (or cities) in the MSA and their population density.

2 Why Poverty Rates and Income and Earnings Distributions Change

A Survey of Explanations

The obvious sources of household income inequality include unequal inherited wealth; unequal wage rates arising from unequal abilities and/or unequal education and training; dispersion in tastes, especially in relative preferences for leisure versus material goods; unequal rates of return on wealth; racial or sexual discrimination in employment and wages; uneven incidence of unemployment; monopolies and monopsonies, such as powerful trade unions, that alter wage rates; and unequal distribution of wage earners across households.[1]

The roles of each of these factors in accounting for income inequality differ in terms of the effects of income inequality on social stability and on the quality of life. Inequality arising from differences in tastes or stages in the life cycle is of a different social and political concern than inequality arising from inherited wealth, discrimination, or institutional practices. The latter reflect characteristics of the macroenvironment that the individual or the household cannot change; it is these sources of inequality that are of primary policy concern.

The research literature on the sources of poverty and of income and earnings inequality for the nation has produced evidence on how the national economic environment contributes. In some cases, the findings are in agreement; in other cases, they conflict. The environmental influences that are studied are seldom those of the immediate (local) economy. In this chapter, I review what we know about how the macro-environment—i.e., demographic structure, characteristics of the labor market (including wages and employment and industrial and market structure), region, and intrametropolitan structure—relates to inequality and poverty.

LOCAL LABOR MARKET EFFECTS ON INCOME DISTRIBUTION AND POVERTY

Because wages and salaries are the principal source of family income, debate over the causes of increases in household income inequality has centered on changes in the labor market, specifically shifts in labor demand, in labor supply, and in institutional regulations. The debate is not about the appropriate conceptual framework. There is consensus on the forces that can account for these phenomena: the facts that earnings have increased more for highly paid workers and less for lower-wage workers must arise either from shifts in labor demand or in labor supply that alter market-determined wages, or from an institutionally induced change in wage-setting practices. There are really two questions at issue in this context: What is the contribution of each of these factors to rising earnings inequality? How does rising earnings inequality affect income inequality?

Sources of Earnings Inequality

Supply Shifts

In their review and evaluation of the research on growing earnings disparity in the nation, Levy and Murnane (1992) cited a simple test of the relative roles of shifts in demand for labor versus shifts in supply of labor in affecting relative wages. If there are two groups of workers, educated and uneducated, and these two groups are the only factors of production, the effects of demand and supply can be distinguished by what Levy and Murnane (p. 1342) call the "Economics 1 Test": "If the group with the slower growing wages is also the group whose numbers grew faster, it suggests wage changes were driven by supply."

In spite of a relative increase in the average level of education and in the proportion of workers who have graduated from college, there is general consensus that the earnings premium placed on skill—represented by education and experience (actually age)—increased during the 1980s, contributing to the growth in earnings inequality. The available evidence indicates that quantity shifts (changes in the proportion of the population with various categories of skill) had greater effects than quality shifts (changes in the quality of the education represented

by a specific level of schooling). Katz and Murphy (1992) demonstrated that the fluctuations in earnings premiums associated with education and age in the 1970s and 1980s can be explained in large part by
the shifts in the relative supply of persons in specific age and education
groups. Bound and Johnson (1991) identified a decrease in the supply
of experienced workers as accounting for increases in the returns on
experience. Topel (1994) found that male wage inequality increased
between 1972 and 1990 because the relative supply of low-skilled
workers increased as a result of an increase in international in-migration and the increased labor force participation of women. He also
found evidence that technological change favored highly skilled workers.

Because there has been increasing inequality of earnings within
skill groups (based on education, age, and gender), most researchers
agree that demand and other sources also contribute.

Demand Shifts

Increases in total labor demand have been linked clearly to
increases in earnings equality. It is well established that the equality of
the earnings distribution is affected by the national business cycle, and
therefore that demand shifts affect the wage distribution. Burtless
(1990) and Moffitt (1990) documented that for the nation, inequality in
male earnings rises with increasing unemployment rates. Burtless
found that a 1 percentage-point rise in the civilian unemployment rate
is associated with a 0.7 percent rise in the Gini coefficient for men's
earnings. There is no similar significant effect for women, however.
Burtless attributes this gender difference to the greater overall variability in work hours per year for women. Because there is less variability
in work hours for men, the decreases caused by unemployment have a
greater effect on earnings inequality.

While the overall level of labor demand (the tightness of the labor
market) influences earnings equality, there is also evidence that there
have been shifts in the nature of the workers demanded, which also
influence the distribution. "Deindustrialization," a term referring to the
relative or absolute decrease in manufacturing employment, is a labor-
demand explanation for the increasing inequality of earnings. Bluestone and Harrison (1986) argued that deindustrialization contributed

to rising inequality, and they used national data to show an increase in the number of persons with low earnings during the 1980s.[2]

It is doubtful, however, that deindustrialization (at least in the sense that the term refers only to declines in manufacturing employment) accounts for increasing earnings inequality. Earnings inequality increased in manufacturing as much as in other industries.[3] Juhn, Murphy, and Pierce (1994), Juhn (1999), and Bound and Johnson (1992) found little growth in industry-specific wage differentials in the 1980s. As Levy and Murnane (1992) concluded, the decline in the relative demand for less-educated workers occurred within industries, most notably in manufacturing. Decreases in the relative demand for less-skilled workers are due more to changes in the technology of production than to industry or product-demand changes.

Several studies have examined the connections between labor demand and income distribution by studying subnational labor markets. Most recently, Partridge, Rickman, and Levernier (1996) analyzed published data on income inequality among families in 1969, 1979, and 1989 in the 48 contiguous U.S. states. Because they studied subnational data, they were able to examine the effects of variation in the macro-environment. They found that the proportion of the state population in metropolitan areas increases inequality. They argued that the urbanized population effect is a combination of economic development and of the role of a larger service sector that rewards high-skilled workers; that is, their finding of an "urbanization effect" is inconsistent with the hypothesis that an increase in total demand (or economic development) reduces earnings inequality, and it supports the hypothesis that deindustrialization increases earnings inequality.

Bartik (1991) studied 89 metropolitan areas between 1979 and 1986 and found that an increase of 1 percent in local employment reduced the long-run local unemployment rate by 0.1 percent, raised the long-run labor force participation rate by 0.1 percent, and increased hourly wages by 0.2 percent. He concluded that increases in the level of local economic development (i.e., higher growth rates) had progressive effects on the distribution of nontransfer income.

From the mid 1970s through mid 1980s, there were several attempts to measure empirically the effects of economic growth (macroeconomic performance) on income inequality in U.S. metropolitan areas. These studies were primarily focused on determining how economic development affects the equality of the income distribution. In these studies, economic development was characterized by population size (to measure economies of scale or extent of monopoly power) and average income. The results showed that increasing intrametropolitan inequality in family income occurred in metropolitan areas with lower median incomes.[4] There was no consensus on the effects of population size.

These studies of metropolitan areas did not resolve how local labor demand influences earnings inequality for several reasons. First, because the studies were all cross-sectional, they could not sort out unmeasured metropolitan characteristics that may be highly correlated with the population or mean income.[5] Second, the studies did not sort out the determinants of earnings inequality (which arises from labor market conditions) from the determinants of family or household income inequality (which arises from the household formation decisions of income producers, as well as earnings inequality among those producers). The equations used in the studies were not correctly specified for sorting out the influences of economic, social, and demographic structures on the earnings distribution versus the same influences on the family or household income distribution. The dependent variable, the distributional measure, was a Gini coefficient computed from household income (rather than individual earnings[6]), although the independent variables (such as industry and occupation of employment, city size, and population density) were labor market characteristics that directly influence the earnings distribution and therefore affect the household income distribution more indirectly. Variables that influence the household income distribution, specifically those that reflect household formation patterns (such as female head of household, household size, and multiple earners or no earners in the household) were frequently excluded. Third, the measures of income inequality were not precisely measured. In many cases, the measures were computed from published aggregations of frequencies of observations within broad income categories, rather than on the basis of the individual incomes and earnings reported in the Public Use Micro Sample of the U.S. Census.

Shifts in Wage-Setting Practices

Changes in wage-setting practices have also been seen as a potential cause of rising inequality. Two institutional changes may be important. First, as unions have historically reduced wage variation, the decreasing role of unions in influencing wage levels may contribute to rising earnings disparity. Second, the new human resource management techniques that emphasize productivity-related compensation such as bonuses, merit increases, and commission-based pay may contribute to earnings dispersion.

Several recent studies (Blackburn, Bloom, and Freeman 1990; Freeman 1996, 1992; Card 1996) using a variety of techniques have estimated that about 20 percent of the increase in earnings inequality in the last 20 years is due to the decrease of collective bargaining as the means of setting wages. Freeman (1996, p. 163) argued that the broader issue is the use of institutional wage-setting practices versus reliance on market forces to determine wages:

> . . . institutions operate on averages; they represent average workers or firms, whereas markets operate on margins; they represent the pressure of supply and demand on the marginal firm/ employee. Institutions are insurance mechanisms for employers and firms; they may reject changes that reduce the well-being of the average employee/firm even though this change fits with the marginal calculus.

Another study provides an example of this point. Card (1989) reported that earnings inequality among pilots, flight attendants, and mechanics within the same firm in the airline industry increased following deregulation of the industry in 1978.

Earnings Inequality and Household Income Inequality

While most studies do not explicitly examine the link between earnings inequality and household income or poverty, those that do so argue for a direct link. Sawhill (1988) concluded from her review of poverty studies that earnings inequality increases poverty. Karoly and Burtless (1995) attributed the growth in family income inequality in the 1979–1989 period, in largest part, to earnings inequality among working men.

Another recent study reported that the relationship between jobs and income distribution may be changing. Blank and Card (1993) demonstrated that the link between the reduction of poverty and economic growth, which is premised on a link between poverty and the availability of jobs offering better wages, has seemingly been reduced as the effects of regional location and family demography have become more significant.

It is quite possible that total employment within many MSAs has increased by adding relatively more low-wage jobs. If these jobs employ persons who previously would not have been employed (that is, persons who would have had no earnings had the employment patterns of prior years persisted), then persons like these newly added workers were not included in the computations of earnings inequality in earlier time periods. Had such persons been included as earners having zero wages, the measures of earnings inequality in the past would have been higher, possibly higher than current levels. If growth in employment, which has been disproportionately in low-wage jobs, has created jobs for persons who previously had no jobs (as opposed to persons who previously had higher-wage jobs), then the increase in wage inequality is not real, but is an artifact of the way inequality is measured.

The argument that persons who previously had zero income (and were "not counted") and now have low positive incomes (and are "counted") inflate estimates of the growth in inequality can only be valid with respect to earnings inequality measures. Earnings (wage/salary) inequality measures are defined with respect to employed individuals; household income inequality measures include the entire population, including those with no income. An expansion of low-wage employment to persons (residing in low-income households) who previously had no wages must reduce household income inequality (unless there are offsetting changes in household formation patterns). In this case, rising earnings inequality could result in decreasing household income inequality.

In sum, recent research on national inequality has clearly demonstrated that increases in the wage premiums placed on skills have contributed to the increase in earnings inequality. The increases in the returns on skills arise from changes in labor supply (i.e., a relative decrease in experienced, educated workers) and from a skill-biased shift in labor demand that appears to arise from skill-biased technological changes. There have also been increases in earnings inequality within skill groups, but there is no consensus on the sources of those increases. There is some agreement that the decline of unionization and collective bargaining agreements has reduced earnings equality.

There is less evidence on how national earnings equality translates into household income equality or poverty rates, and the evidence that exists does not clearly demonstrate the connections for the nation. No one has addressed the issue for metropolitan areas.

These findings for the nation do not translate into clear expectations about how intermetropolitan variations in earnings inequality or in household income inequality and poverty are affected by changes in the distribution of education and skills among workers or by changes in industrial composition. Even if there is a "shortage" of a particular skill group within a metropolitan area, intermetropolitan migration is expected to attract workers with these skills, reducing wage differentials both with respect to other metropolitan areas and with respect to other groups within the metropolitan area, thus reducing inequality. Intermetropolitan mobility of workers acts to reduce regional differentials in wages so that differences in proportions or quantities of workers with a given set of skills or education levels may not affect the measured level of earnings inequality within a metropolitan area. If this is the case, and if within-MSA income equality is a better measure of the desired equality of outcomes than national income inequality, then the growing inequality within the nation that is attributable to changes in the national demand for and supply of skilled workers may not be of policy concern.

Intermetropolitan variations in earnings inequality will persist, however, if they arise from a production process that is based on immobile inputs. For example, metropolitan areas with natural resource endowments that are complementary to production with low-skilled workers will have relatively more low-wage workers. For example, if climate or beaches or mountains attract tourists and if the tourist industry creates more low-skill jobs, then tourist-serving MSAs will have more earnings inequality. The wage distribution effects of industrial differences will also depend on the extent to which markets versus institutions are used to set wages within the MSA.

EFFECTS OF DEMOGRAPHICS ON INCOME
DISTRIBUTION AND POVERTY

There are a variety of ways that the demographic characteristics of the population may affect or be affected by income and earnings distributions. Some characteristics that individuals cannot alter (such as race, gender, or age) affect income or earnings distributions if they affect productivity or perceptions of productivity, or if there is social or economic discrimination with respect to such characteristics. Inequality associated with these characteristics is of policy concern.

Studies of income inequality within metropolitan areas have found that areas having a larger proportion of African Americans,[7] a larger proportion of families headed by women,[8] or a larger proportion of households headed by persons over age 65[9] have more household income inequality.

Demographic characteristics that individuals or households are able to change, such as household composition or labor force participation decisions, also affect income and earnings distributions. For example, decreases in the proportion of adults who are married increase the proportion of adults and children who live in households with one or no earners. Increases in the labor force participation and work hours of married women increase the proportion of adults (and, depending on the numbers of children of employed versus unemployed women, may decrease the proportion of children) in households with two or more earners. To the extent that the number of earners affects household income and the number of hours affects wages, these changes in earners per household potentially alter the household distribution of income and the distribution of earnings among workers.

Karoly and Burtless (1995) attributed rising family inequality for the nation between 1979 and 1989 in part to the positive correlation between women's earnings and family income. Levy (1989) and Juhn and Murphy (1992) also found that earnings and employment growth have been greatest for the wives of high-wage men.

Most studies have found that increases in households headed solely by women contribute to rising household income inequality and poverty. Sawhill (1988), in her review of the poverty literature, cited numerous studies that demonstrate the importance of increases in female-headed households. Karoly and Burtless (1995) attributed about 25 percent of the growth of inequality in family income between 1979 and 1989 to changes in family composition, especially the increase in the proportion of families headed by a single woman. Partridge, Rickman, and Levernier (1996) reached similar conclusions studying family income inequality in the 48 contiguous U.S. states in 1969, 1979, and 1989. Gottschalk and Danziger (1993) argued, however, that the potential effects of rising proportions of female-headed households on poverty rates were offset by the decreasing numbers of children in those households.

Previous research leads us to expect that the demographic composition of metropolitan areas may affect income distribution and poverty rates. Households headed by men or couples are expected to have more income as the result of gender differences in earnings and the potential for more earners in households with more adults. The proportion of households headed by African Americans or retired persons may also have an effect on overall equality.

LOCATION EFFECTS: REGIONAL AND INTRAMETROPOLITAN

Regional Variation in the United States

There is evidence that geographic disparities in household income and in individual earnings have been increasing across a broad range of geographic units, including between U.S. census regions and within U.S. metropolitan areas.

Recent data show increases in income disparity across U.S. census regions since the late 1970s, as average income levels on the East and West coasts (especially since 1982) increased relative to the levels in other regions (see Eberts 1989).[10] This trend is particularly surprising in the historical context. Except for the 1920 to 1940 period (Nourse 1968), there had been continuous convergence in regional income levels between 1870 and 1979; since 1979, however, there has been increasing disparity. Browne (1989) argued that earnings are the principal component of the divergence. Eberts (1989) and Farber and

Newman (1987) attributed the divergence in earnings by region to differences in the returns on worker's skills. Carlino (1986), Gerking and Weirick (1983), and Roback (1982), among others, have argued that amenity differences between regions also contribute to wage differences. Barro and Sala-i-Martin (1992) found that the recent divergence in state incomes can be attributed to sectoral composition or industry differences.

Getis (1988) documented a growing income disparity at a more finely delineated regional level, that of cities and their suburbs. Reich (1991) cited increasing intrametropolitan residential segmentation by income. Mayer (1996) reported that, in 1964, an American family in the lowest fifth of the income distribution was 1.2 times more likely than the average family in the metropolitan area to live in the central city, and that this ratio has grown gradually over 30 years to a high of almost 1.4 times by 1994.

These geographic studies have mostly focused, however, on changes in the distribution of income between (as opposed to within) regions. Karoly and Klerman (1992) found that the rising disparity between regions accounts for about 5 percent of the increasing disparity among families nationwide. Unlike the other geographic studies, however, Karoly and Klerman also examined intra-regional disparity within U.S. census regions and found that income inequality had also increased within each region.

Nielsen and Alderson (1997) analyzed family income inequality within U.S. counties for 1970, 1980, and 1990. They found that economic growth decreases family income inequality within counties, although the effect is lessening due to increasing inequality in the most prosperous counties. They also found that increases in female labor force participation decreases inequality and that increasing educational inequality increases inequality. The study does not address the issues raised here because it uses counties rather than MSAs and families rather than households. (As discussed in Chapter 1 and in Chapter 4, counties are a problematic observational unit because the boundaries are not drawn with respect to market activity. Families are a problematic unit because they exclude persons who do not reside with relatives, a phenomenon that may strongly affect the distribution of income among individuals.)

The most recent analyses of intermetropolitan variation in income distribution are those of Cloutier (1997) and Galster, McCorkhill, and Gopalan (1988). The Cloutier study, of changes in the distribution of family income within 216 metropolitan areas between 1980 and 1990, found that most of the increase in inequality was accounted for by increases in the inequality of the distribution of education, in the proportion of female-headed families, and in the proportion of metropolitan area jobs in the managerial/professional occupations, and by decreases in the size of the manufacturing and public sectors. He also found that increases in the number of workers per family decreased the growth of inequality.

While Cloutier addressed many of the same issues I study here, there are important differences. Cloutier analyzed the distribution of family income, rather than household income or poverty rates, and he used an approximation of income inequality that underestimates the true variation in income (to be discussed below). Although there has been a substantial decline in the proportion of the population living in families and this proportion differs among MSAs, Cloutier does not account for these differences over time or between MSAs in the selection of the population into families. Because Cloutier excludes a substantial proportion of the MSA population from his study, it is difficult to evaluate his results. Cloutier's analysis of family income inequality suffers from the same problem of selective exclusion of the population that complicates the interpretation of studies of changing wage/salary distributions.

Galster, McCorkhill, and Gopalan found that the proportion of metropolitan area jobs in nonproduction sectors, the proportions of the population aged 18 to 34 and over 65, and the female proportion of the workforce were the predominant forces increasing household income inequality within 120 metropolitan areas in 1980. Population was of marginal statistical significance and bore an inverted-U-shaped relationship to inequality, increasing inequality with rising population followed by decreasing inequality. Because the study combines data on the workforce with data on the entire residential population and uses household income (rather than earnings) as the distributional variable, the study does not resolve any of the issues raised here.

Both the Galster and the Cloutier studies compute the measure of inequality (the Gini coefficient) on the basis of published aggregations by income category, rather than on the basis of the individual incomes and earnings reported in the Public Use Micro Sample. The use of such aggregations results in systematically lower estimations of inequality than when inequality is computed using individual data.

Intrametropolitan Location

Relatively recent literature has examined the links between residential or neighborhood locations and income and earnings. Abramson, Tobin, and VanderGoot (1995) reported an 8.1 percent increase in the extent to which the poor were isolated in the 100 largest MSAs between 1980 and 1990.[11] They also found that the poor are more isolated in those metropolitan areas with larger representations of African Americans in their population. Kasarda (1993) also found increased concentrations of poverty in the largest metropolitan areas for the same time period. Cutler and Glaeser (1997) concluded that a 13 percent reduction in residential race segregation in U.S. metropolitan areas in 1990 would eliminate one-third of the income gap between whites and blacks, mostly by increasing black income. They found weak evidence of a small positive influence on white income. Racial segregation appears to have diminished slightly in the same period, however, as reported by Abramson, Tobin, and VanderGoot (1995) for their 100 MSAs (and in Chapter 3 of this study).

There is much agreement that racial segregation affects job outcomes (e.g., Massey and Denton 1993; Ihlanfeldt 1992). Fears that racial discrimination in housing contributes to greater spatial concentration or isolation for poor African-American households has motivated a substantial portion of the research. The mechanisms by which location can influence poverty and inequality are more controversial.

John Kain (1968) argued that a "spatial mismatch" between workers' residences and job sites increased unemployment rates for urban ghetto residents. He developed the" spatial mismatch" hypothesis, which states that housing discrimination restricts African-American residential locations to inner-city ghettos, which in turn inhibits their ability to obtain employment in the suburbs, where metropolitan job growth is concentrated. This spatial mismatch is thought to account for at least part of the higher unemployment rates and lower earnings of African Americans in metropolitan areas. Kain's analysis of employment and residential data from Detroit and Chicago in the

1950s led him to conclude that housing discrimination reduced non-white employment by 9,000 in Detroit and 24,000 in Chicago.

William Julius Wilson (1987) wrote of the "urban underclass," arguing that the social isolation of ghetto residents has increased as the African-American middle class has moved into suburban and/or more-integrated, higher-income neighborhoods.[12] This social isolation is argued to produce externalities for ghetto residents by increasing unemployment, decreasing earnings and household income, and escalating social pathologies among residents beyond those that would have occurred in a neighborhood with a more economically and socially diverse population.   As with the spatial mismatch hypothesis, the urban underclass hypothesis also attributes some of the unfavorable income and labor market outcomes for ghetto residents to housing discrimination, but the underlying mechanisms differ.   Under the urban underclass hypothesis, it is the social/economic climate of the neighborhood (for example, the lack of employed persons to serve as role models or informants about job opportunities; the presence of disruptive persons who increase crime and make the provision of services, including public education, more difficult, and often decreasing the quality of that available) and not its physical distance from job sites that contribute to higher unemployment, lower earnings, and lower household incomes of ghetto residents.

The agreement that residential segmentation and economic outcomes are linked has not led to agreement on these two hypotheses, however.   Recent reviews of the empirical research testing these two hypotheses demonstrate a lack of consensus on their validity.   Ihlanfeldt (1992), Kain (1992), and Holzer (1991) have reviewed the evidence for the spatial mismatch hypothesis and document the lack of consensus.   Jencks and Mayer (1990) document the lack of consensus on the urban underclass hypothesis after an extensive review of the evidence.

A variety of studies have explored the ways that segregation affects the working of the economy.   Benabou (1993) argued that segregation is socially costly because it eliminates spillovers between highly skilled and less-skilled individuals.   Crane (1991), Case and Katz (1991), and Borjas (1995) showed an empirical relationship between where people live, who they associate with, and their quality of life. Manski (1993) argued, however, that it is difficult (if not impossible) to obtain reliable empirical measurements of such neighborhood effects.[13] One problem is that the observed correlations between neighborhood of residence and economic outcomes do not establish cause and effect. People may live in ghettos because they have not succeeded in the labor market, or they may not succeed in the labor market because they live in ghettos. Another problem is that ghettos, racial segregation, and income segmentation may hurt everyone's economic opportunities, both residents of poor areas and residents of richer areas, because these phenomena interfere with the quality of the match between worker characteristics and job requirements. If that is the case, then a comparison of ghetto residents with non-ghetto residents does not identify the loss.

O'Regan and Quigley (1996) have directly tested whether the social and economic characteristics of a neighborhood's residents or its physical proximity to jobs better explain the labor-market outcomes of neighborhood residents. Based on intra-urban variation of census tract characteristics for four New Jersey metropolitan areas (Newark, Bergen-Passaic, Middlesex, and Monmouth), they found much stronger effects of neighborhood social and economic characteristics than they did of job proximity in determining youth employment.

Cutler and Glaeser (1997) examined the effects of residential segregation across the 209 largest MSAs in 1990. By examining the effects of residential segregation on a variety of social and economic outcomes for persons aged 20–24 and 25–30, and using a series of instrumental variables to identify causality, they found support for both the underclass and spatial mismatch hypotheses. They also found a substantial unexplained residual for each of these outcomes.

In summary, although the correlation between racial segregation, income segmentation, and poor job outcomes that contribute to low incomes and poverty is well established for individuals, the mechanisms that account for the correlation are not understood. The evidence on correlation among individuals needs to be supplemented by evidence that explores whether MSAs with more racial segregation have higher poverty rates, higher concentrations of poverty in the central city, and greater income and earnings inequality.

SUMMARY

There are no studies that have examined changes in household income inequality or earnings inequality among MSAs. Although there are numerous studies of the national change in household income inequality, few have sorted out the effects of changes in earnings equality from the effects caused by other sources.

Prior research does provide guidance on which characteristics of MSAs are likely to be related to changes in inequality. Obviously, the labor market (including both changes in wages and in employment) and demographic shifts (including race, age, and changes in household structures) must be investigated. The geography and structure of the MSA, including population and indicators of race and income segmentation, are also potential correlates of changes in household income inequality and earnings inequality.

Notes

1. Blinder (1974) articulated much of this listing.
2. This study spawned much debate and research, including Blackburn and Bloom (1987), Burtless (1990), Gottschalk and Moffitt (1994), and Kosters and Ross (1987, 1988).
3. Table 3.1 shows that earnings inequality increased, on average, by 4.0 percent among blue-collar men in MSAs during the 1980s, compared with 4.1 percent among professionals/managers and 2.7 percent among salesworkers of both genders for the same time period. Earnings inequality actually declined in the producer service industry.
4. See Farbman (1975), Danziger (1976), Nord (1980a, 1980b), and Haworth et al. (1978, 1982). Garofalo and Fogarty (1979) found a U-shaped relationship, with inequality declining through some income range, reaching a minimum, and then increasing as median income increased.
5. See Chapter 4 for a discussion of this problem.
6. An exception to this is Long, Rasmussen, and Haworth (1977) who presented an analysis using income of males for 1969 (but not restricted to earnings).
7. See Farbman (1975), Danziger (1976), Nord (1980a, 1980b), Haworth et al. (1979, 1980), and Garofalo and Fogarty (1979), for example.
8. See Nord (1980a, 1980b), Galster, McCorkhill, and Gopalan (1988), Nielsen and Alderson (1997), and Cloutier (1997), for example.
9. See Garofalo and Fogarty (1979) and Galster, McCorkhill, And Gopalan (1988), for example. Nielsen and Alderson (1997), in their study of income inequality within U.S. countries, found that the proportion of the population over age 65

increased inequality in 1970, had no effect in 1980, and increased inequality in 1990 cross-sectional analyses.

10. Dickie and Gerking (1988) have summarized the rather extensive research on earnings differentials across U.S. regions.

11. Actually, they reported the indexes: 19.7 for 1980 and 21.3 for 1990.

12. Mayer (1996) found that high-income African Americans have been leaving central cities at rates comparable to those of whites since the later 1960s, but that the concentration of high-income African Americans in the central city remains about 30 percent above that of other U.S. families.

13. Neighborhood effects occur when the propensity of an individual to behave in some way—e.g., to be poor—varies with the prevalence of that behavior in a reference group containing the individual, such as the residential neighborhood.

3   The Data and the Variables

A central problem in trying to understand the effects of the macro-environment, or the structure of the economy, on rising inequality in earnings and income and on increasing poverty rates has been the lack of data points. Because the data for most scholarly studies of income distribution are national time-series data, the empirical evidence for correlation between characteristics of the macro-environment and changes in income distribution have been based on statistical analyses of data sets that often include only 25 to 50 annual observations, or on a handful of observations of measures of inequality that are compared with a handful of changes in the labor market or in demographic circumstances. In this chapter, we examine income inequality and poverty in U.S. metropolitan areas.

THE DATA

The 5 percent Public Use Micro Samples (PUMS) of the 1980 and the 1990 U.S. censuses provide data on the earnings, income, demographic characteristics, household characteristics, labor market characteristics, and metropolitan locations of individuals. These data on individuals permit one to compute, for each metropolitan area (MSA), measures of the inequality of the distribution of earnings for individuals and of income for households or families; they also permit the computation of inequality measures for subpopulations within each MSA. The data used for this study are from the 182 largest U.S. MSAs in 1980 and 1990;[1] data on earnings and income reflect the experiences of respondents in the prior calendar year (i.e., 1979 for 1980 census data).

Gini Coefficients

Figures 3.1a and 3.1b illustrate the patterns of earnings inequality and household income inequality across selected U.S. MSAs in 1989. The measure of inequality used in these figures is the Gini coefficient.[2] Figure 3.1a shows earnings inequality and household income inequal-

Figure 3.1a MSAs with Similar Household Income Inequality and Earnings Inequality, 1989

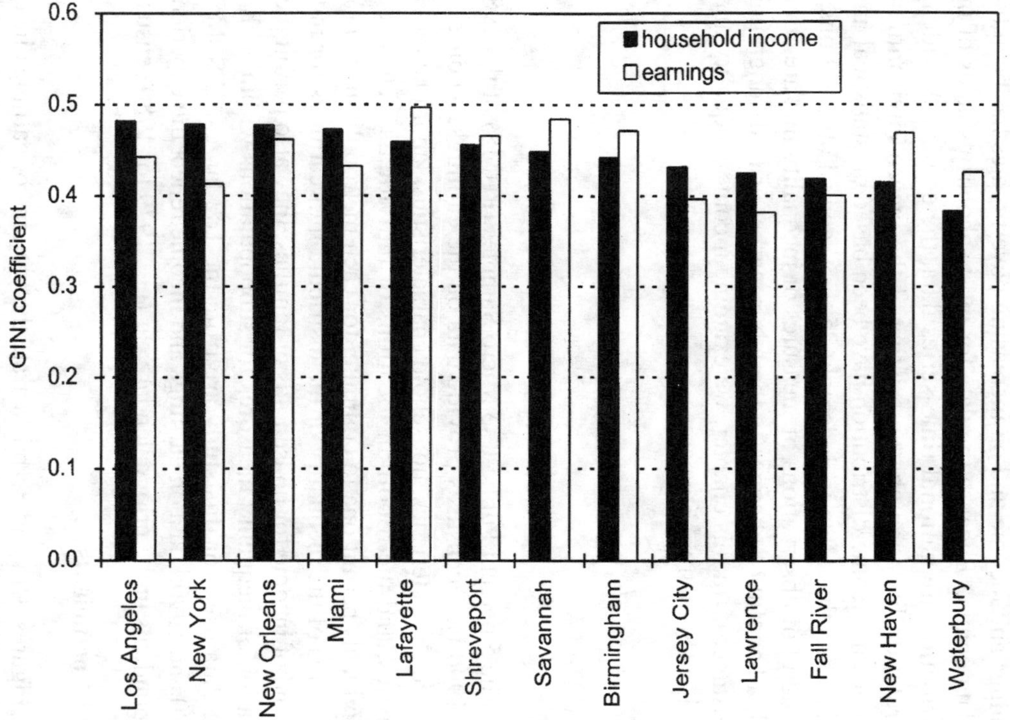

Figure 3.1b MSAs with Larger Differences between Household Income Inequality and Earnings Inequality, 1989

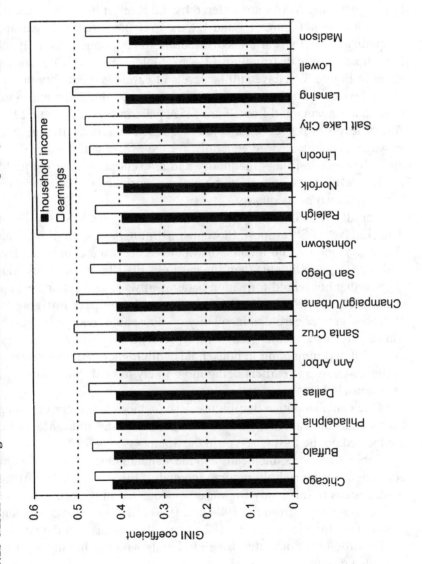

ity in 1989 for selected MSAs in which these two measures have similar values; Figure 3.1b shows the same measures for selected MSAs in which there are greater differences between these two measures. In both figures, the MSAs are ordered by the level of household income inequality. As in Figures 1.1 and 1.2, the irregular variation of earnings inequality shows that earnings distributions do not translate simply into household income distributions. For example, New York City and Fall River in Figure 3.1a have similar levels of earnings inequality but different levels of household income inequality. Johnstown and Santa Cruz, and Lansing and Lowell are MSA pairs in Figure 3.1b that have similar levels of household income inequality, but very different levels of wage inequality. More generally, for the MSAs with greater differences between earnings inequality and household income inequality (Figure 3.1b), there appears to be greater earnings inequality and less household income inequality.

For all the MSAs in Figure 3.1b, but only for six MSAs in Figure 3.1a (Lafayette, Shreveport, Savannah, Birmingham, New Haven, and Waterbury), household income distributions are more equal (i.e., have a lower Gini coefficient) than the earnings distributions. These data suggest that household formation patterns of wage earners or the labor force participation decisions of household members mitigate the effects of greater earnings inequality on household income inequality. These patterns are consistent with lower-end wage earners (such as young adults) remaining in households with higher-end wage earners, or higher-end wage earners being more likely to be the sole earners in their households.

One can also notice that Figure 3.1b includes a number of college towns and state capitals, while Figure 3.1a includes more MSAs that are located on the East Coast or in the South.

Table 3.1 reports the means and the standard deviations of the Gini coefficient for household income inequality for all of the 182 metropolitan areas in this study for various income/earnings categories and population groups, from the 1980 and 1990 censuses. The coefficients reported are the means for the 182 metropolitan areas, not the national Gini coefficients computed for individuals who are members of the identified groups.

Table 3.1 MSA Gini Coefficients for Household Income and Individual Earnings

Category	Mean	Standard deviation	Highest value	Lowest value
Household income				
1979	0.374	0.026	0.439 New York NY	0.294 Lowell MA
1989	0.412	0.026	0.488 McAllen TX	0.360 York PA
change[a] (%)	10.6	4.9	0.279 Lowell MA	-0.024 Stockton CA
Earnings				
All earners				
1979	0.453	0.020	0.535 Provo UT	0.398 Fall River MA
1989	0.466	0.022	0.537 Provo UT	0.382 Waterbury CT
change (%)	2.7	3.3	0.101 Pittsburgh PA	-0.089 Bridgeport CT
Full-time, year-round				
1979	0.316	0.020	0.370 Stamford CT	0.269 Duluth MN / Lawrence MA
1989	0.338	0.023	0.405 Stamford CT	0.265 Lawrence MA
change (%)	7.1	4.4	0.203 Green Bay WI	-0.081 New Haven CT
All men				
1979	0.404	0.031	0.522 Gainesville FL	0.332 Lorain OH
1989	0.442	0.030	0.537 Gainesville FL	0.342 Waterbury CT
change (%)	9.4	5.3	0.240 Racine WI	-0.073 New Haven CT

(continued)

Table 3.1 (continued)

Category	Mean	Standard deviation	Highest value	Lowest value
Blue-collar men				
1979	0.333	0.033	0.457 Gainesville FL	0.254 Gary IN
1989	0.346	0.028	0.426 McAllen TX	0.284 York PA
change (%)	4.0	6.6	0.198 Lorain OH	-0.138 New Haven CT
All women				
1979	0.435	0.021	0.519 Provo UT	0.380 Fall River MA
1989	0.441	0.023	0.510 Provo UT	0.388 Fall River MA
change (%)	1.4	3.1	0.117 Beaumont TX	-0.079 Atlantic City NJ
Clerical women				
1979	0.363	0.023	0.463 Provo UT	0.308 Fall River MA
1989	0.364	0.025	0.451 Provo UT	0.308 Lawrence MA
change (%)	0.3	4.7	0.152 Lima OH	-0.157 St. Cloud MN
Earners aged 25–34				
1979	0.366	0.018	0.437 Chico CA	0.323 Fall River MA
1989	0.372	0.023	0.455 Salt Lake City UT	0.320 Waterbury CT
change (%)	1.5	4.9	0.197 Flint MI	-0.120 Atlantic City NJ
Whites				
1979	0.452	0.020	0.534 Provo UT	0.398 Fall River MA Jersey City NJ

1989	0.463	0.022	0.536 Provo UT	0.376 Waterbury CT
change (%)	2.5	3.2	0.099 Pittsburgh PA	−0.093 Bridgeport CT
African Americans				
1979	0.432	0.045	0.621 Jackson MI	0.243 Fall River MA
1989	0.449	0.044	0.593 Eugene OR	0.314 Fall River MA
change (%)	4.7	10.8	0.605 Richland WA	−0.370 Provo UT
Professionals/managers				
1979	0.399	0.021	0.464 Provo UT	0.327 Lawrence MA
1989	0.416	0.025	0.472 Chico CA	0.306 Waterbury CT
change (%)	4.1	4.7	0.190 Racine WI	−0.117 Waterbury CT
Salesworkers				
1979	0.533	0.021	0.613 Gainesville FL	0.471 Albany NY
1989	0.547	0.022	0.604 Ann Arbor MI	0.475 Waterbury CT
change (%)	2.7	4.2	0.150 Macon GA	−0.144 Waterbury CT
Producer services				
1979	0.515	0.026	0.574 Flint MI	0.404 Reno NV
1989	0.506	0.030	0.571 Flint MI	0.380 Reno NV
change (%)	−1.7	3.8	0.125 Alexandria LA	−0.156 Atlantic City NJ

[a] The change rows are computed by taking the mean of the change rates for all MSAs in the study. The MSA change rate is computed by subtracting the 1980 mean income or earnings for the category in the MSA from the 1990 mean and dividing this difference by the 1980 mean.

The category with the most equal distribution within the metropolitan areas—i.e., the lowest mean Gini coefficient reported on Table 3.1 (0.316)—is the 1979 earnings income for full-time, year-round workers. At least part of the reason for less variation in income among full-time, year-round workers is that there is less variation in total hours worked. The category with the most unequal distribution (0.547) is the 1989 earnings income of salesworkers. Salesworkers have greater variation in earnings because they include workers with more variation in hours (i.e., more part-time workers) and more variation in skills (the occupation includes those who sell candy and those who sell office buildings).

The data in Table 3.1 confirm the patterns suggested by Figure 3.1. Other than for full-time year-round workers, household income distributions are more equal within MSAs than are the earnings distributions. Household formation patterns and/or the labor supply decisions of household members apparently mitigate the effects of earnings inequality on household income.

Focusing on Selected MSAs to Illustrate the Issues

Figures 3.2a–c illustrate the 10-year rates of change in household income inequality and in earnings inequality in selected MSAs between 1979 and 1989; the panels were selected to illustrate patterns of earnings and household inequality change across three different sets of MSAs. Figure 3.2a includes MSAs selected because the two rates of change were more similar than in other MSAs. Note that in Norfolk, Virginia, there was slight convergence in both household income and earnings. Figure 3.2b shows the same measures for MSAs selected from the Mid-Atlantic region. While Philadelphia and New York City show a growth in household income inequality that is slightly greater than that in earnings inequality, the other MSAs show substantially greater growth in household income inequality, both relative to the same measure in Philadelphia and New York City and relative to their own changes in earnings inequality.

Figure 3.2c shows these measures of inequality for smaller MSAs selected for divergence in the two rates of change.

Figure 3.2a 10-Year Rates of Change in Household Income and Earnings Inequality (1979–1989), Group A

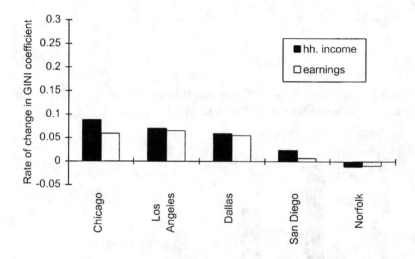

Figure 3.2b 10-Year Rates of Change in Household Income and Earnings Inequality (1979–1989), Group B

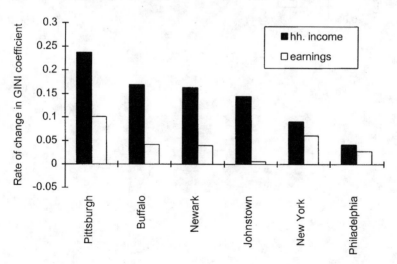

**Figure 3.2c 10-Year Rates of Change in Household Income and Earnings
Inequality (1979–1989), Group C**

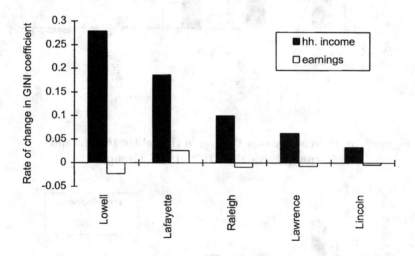

Lowell, Massachusetts, experienced the greatest decrease in earnings inequality on the chart, but it also had the greatest increase in household income inequality. All of the MSAs on this chart had very little change in earnings inequality, but their household income inequality growth ranged widely.

Unlike the comparisons of the 1989 inequality levels in Figures 3.1a and b, there are no obvious differences between the MSAs that had their rates of earnings and household income inequality move together and those that had widely different shifts in those two measures of inequality. As noted in the discussion of Figures 1.1 and 1.2, those that had widely divergent changes in income and earnings inequality include large and small MSAs as well as western, eastern, midwestern, and southern MSAs.

What accounts for the differences in how household income inequality changed between these three sets of MSAs? It cannot be changes in the distribution of wages. This study will develop and statistically test explanations of the variation in income inequality among all 182 MSAs, and I will return to these three figures for illustration.

The metropolitan Gini coefficients for each income group listed in Table 3.1 grew, on average, between 1979 and 1989. Household income had the greatest increase in inequality, relative to the other Gini values listed. The average metropolitan area experienced a 10.6 percent increase in its household income Gini between 1979 and 1989. The largest percentage increase occurred in Lowell, Massachusetts (where the 1979 index was the lowest among MSAs), rising by 27.9 percent; the smallest increase—in fact a decrease in inequality—occurred in Stockton, California, where the index changed by –2.4 percent. While the distribution of wage earners among households mitigates the effects of earnings inequality, the extent of this mitigation diminished during the 1980s: household income inequality increased 10.6 percent, while earnings inequality increased only 2.7 percent.

The mean earnings Gini increased more for full-time, year-round workers (7.1 percent), and less for workers aged 25 to 34 (1.5 percent). Men experienced a faster growth in earnings inequality than women, 9.4 percent vs. 1.4 percent, and African Americans experienced more rapid growth than whites, 4.7 percent vs. 2.5 percent. The rate of growth in earnings inequality varied across occupations. Professionals/managers and men in blue-collar jobs experienced increases of 4.1 percent and 4.0 percent, respectively while women clerical workers experienced essentially no change and the wages of workers in producer service industries became more equal (a 1.7 percent decline in inequality).

The standard deviation values on Table 3.1 index the extent to which local markets differ in their relative equality or inequality and in the rate and direction of change in inequality. There is greater variation (larger standard deviation) among MSAs in the household income inequality than in earnings inequality. There is greater variation among MSAs in male wages than in female wages, while younger workers (aged 25–34) experience less variation than other age groups. The greatest variation in earnings inequality among MSAs occurs for African-American wage earners.

Poverty Rates

There is also substantial variation among MSAs and within MSAs (cities versus suburbs) in another important measure of income distribution, the poverty rate. In 1969, 13.7 percent of the U.S. population had incomes below the poverty line. This rate dropped to 12.4 percent in 1979 but increased to 13.1 percent by 1989. Table 3.2 reports the variation in poverty rates in central cities and in MSAs. In 1979, 11.7 percent of persons in the average MSA had incomes below the poverty line, growing to 12.7 percent in 1989. Poverty rates in central cities were higher; an average of 15.9 percent in 1979 and 18.5 percent in 1989. The highest poverty rate in 1989 for the 182 largest MSAs was in McAllen, Texas, and for central cities, in Benton Harbor, Michigan. In 1989, the lowest poverty rate for an MSA with a central city was for Stamford, Connecticut, at 6.3 percent; but the poverty rates within central cities have exceeded both the national rate and the rate for the MSA they are part of in both 1979 and 1989.

Table 3.2 Mean and Standard Deviation of 1979 and 1989 Metropolitan Poverty Rates

Area	Mean	Standard deviation	Highest value	Lowest value
MSA				
1979 poverty rate (%)	11.7	4.03	35.2 McAllen TX	5.4 Stamford CT
1989 poverty rate (%)	12.7	5.03	41.9 McAllen TX	4.2 Nassau NY
change (%)	9.3	19.07	68 Lafayette LA	−28 Atlantic City NJ
Central city				
1979 poverty rate (%)	15.9	5.15	38.7 Benton Harbor MI	7.0 Appleton WI[a]
1989 poverty rate (%)	18.5	6.45	58.0 Benton Harbor MI	6.3 Stamford CT[a]
change (%)	17.6	20.95	81 Flint MI	26 Wilmington DE
Central city to MSA ratio				
1979 poverty rate	1.41	0.40	3.19 Hartford CT	0.83 McAllen TX
1989 poverty rate	1.53	0.50	3.94 Benton Harbor MI	0.86 McAllen TX
change (%)	0.07	0.07	0.31 St. Cloud MN	−0.18 Lafayette LA

[a] The lowest rate for an MSA having a central city. Because Nassau, New York, has no central city, there can be no poverty rate in the central city of metropolitan Nassau.

Poverty Rates and Income Inequality

Figures 3.3a–c illustrate the 1989 poverty rate for all persons and its change as a percentage of the 1979 value for each of the MSAs in Figures 3.2a–c; the MSA with the largest change in household income inequality appears at the left side of each figure and the MSA with the smallest change is at the right.

Figure 3.3a shows that the pattern of poverty and change in these MSAs is similar to the MSA changes in household and earnings inequality (Figure 3.2a). These MSAs had similar levels of poverty in 1989, with some variation in the change over the previous decade. The two MSAs with the least growth in household inequality, San Diego and Norfolk, also had the least growth in poverty: Norfolk experienced a decrease in poverty, and San Diego experienced no change in poverty. Chicago, Los Angeles, and Dallas had slight increases in poverty, just as they had slight increases in earnings and household income inequality.

Figure 3.3b shows a pattern of 1989 poverty rates similar to those on Figure 3.3a, but with much greater variability in the percentage of change in poverty and a less-apparent relationship between the change in the poverty rate and the earnings or household income inequality (Figure 3.2b). Newark and Johnstown, in particular, have changes in poverty that are "out of line" with the changes in household income inequality.

Figure 3.3c shows an even more puzzling pattern. Figure 3.2c showed these small MSAs to have little increase in earnings inequality and significant variation in the rate of change in household income inequality, but nothing there helps us understand why Lafayette, Louisiana, and Lincoln, Nebraska, had sizeable increases in their poverty rates relative to the other three MSAs.

What accounts for these different experiences in poverty in the 1980s among these MSAs? Is it jobs and wages? If so, why don't the changes in earnings inequality track changes in poverty or household income inequality?

Figure 3.3a 1989 Poverty Rate and 1979–1989 Changes: Group A

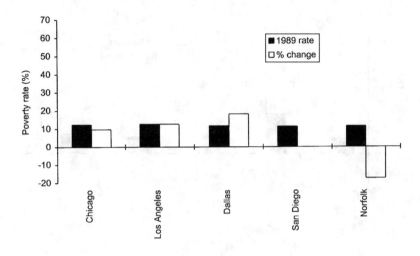

Figure 3.3b 1989 Poverty Rate and 1979–1989 Changes: Group B

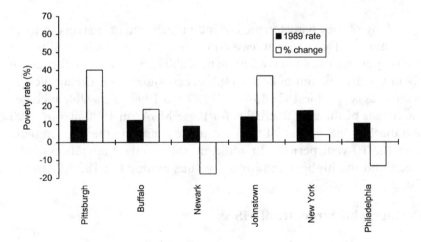

Figure 3.3c 1989 Poverty Rate and 1979–1989 Changes: Group C

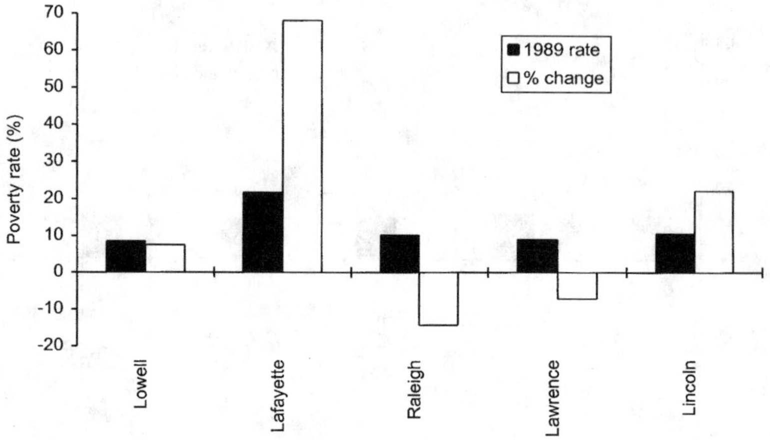

ECONOMIC AND SOCIAL CHARACTERISTICS

Many of the characteristics of individuals and of markets or local economies that affect (or at least correlate with) income inequality and higher poverty rates are well known. Table 3.3 provides information about the distribution of demographic, economic, and structural characteristics across the 182 MSAs in 1980 and 1990. This table includes the means of the characteristics for these MSAs in 1980 and in 1990 and the 182-MSA mean of the percentage change in the characteristic over the 10-year period. In addition, the standard deviation of the mean and the highest and lowest values among the 182 MSAs are listed.

Demographic Structure of MSAs

Several demographic characteristics of individuals are associated with their personal income levels and therefore with poverty or income levels of households. It does not necessarily follow, however, that MSAs with larger proportions of persons whose characteristics are associated with low income or high likelihoods of poverty have higher poverty rates or more unequal income distributions. If these characteristics have more to do with how income is distributed among individuals rather than with the overall productivity of the local economy, then having more persons with the "individual characteristics" associated with poverty or low income will have little effect on the MSA poverty rate or the overall level of inequality. In this case, the demographic structure of the MSA population (such as race or age composition) would not be associated with the MSA poverty rate or income inequality, even though such characteristics might well identify the rank ordering of households or individuals in the income distribution. Age, race, and household formation patterns—represented by the gender of the householder and the number of earners in a household—are associated with individual and household poverty rates and low income, but their effects on overall MSA poverty rates depend on their association with the productivity of the local economy.

Migration provides an interesting example of a demographic phenomenon that is positively correlated with the productivity of the local economy but negatively associated with individual income. Other things held equal, persons who have recently changed their MSA of residence have lower incomes than those who are longer-duration residents. MSAs that attract in-migrants from other areas are usually experiencing more economic growth, however. Economic growth generally has greater effects on lower-income persons and therefore is associated with a decrease in poverty rates. The net relationship between in-migration and metropolitan measures of income inequality or poverty rates is difficult to predict *a priori*. Because in-migrants are disproportionately attracted to growing MSAs and because economic growth generally favors lower income groups, MSAs with more in-migration may actually have less poverty and income inequality, even though in-migrants have lower incomes than nonmigrants.

There is substantial variation in demographic structure among MSAs. Table 3.3 shows that the rate of in-migration to MSAs was relatively constant, with 18.0 percent of residents in 1990[3] being new to the area in the last five years, versus 18.9 percent in 1980 (although some areas, such as Saginaw, Michigan, experienced substantial increases in in-migration). The connections between in-migration rates and economic expansion are illustrated by Richland, Washington, which had the greatest drop in the rate of in-migration and the slowest

Table 3.3 1980 and 1990 MSA Characteristics

Characteristics	Mean	Standard deviation	Highest value	Lowest value
Demographic[a]				
Female-headed hh.[b]				
1980 (%)	28.0	3.6	39 New York NY	17 Richland WA
1990 (%)	32.0	3.8	44 Macon GA	21 Provo UT
change (%)[c]	15.3	8.6	76 Lowell MA	-4 Green Bay WI
No-earner hh.				
1980 (%)	15.0	4.7	38 Sarasota FL	7 Lowell MA
1990 (%)	15.0	4.7	34 Sarasota FL	10 Raleigh NC
change (%)	7.3	14.7	68 Richland WA	-29 Stockton CA
Multiple-earner hh.				
1980 (%)	52.0	5.1	64 Lowell MA	34 Sarasota FL
1990 (%)	54.0	5.1	67 Madison WI	40 Sarasota FL
change (%)	6.8	5.4	23 Stockton CA	-12 Lafayette LA
African-American pop.				
1980 (%)	9.2	8.5	45 Jackson MS	0 Provo UT
1990 (%)	11.0	10.0	51 Jackson MS	0 Provo UT
change (%)	27.9	37.2	201 Lawrence MA	-38 Huntington WV
Elderly hh. head[d]				
1980 (%)	7.6	2.0	40 Bradenton FL	9 Fayetteville NC

1990 (%)	20.4	42	Sarasota FL	12	Fayetteville NC
change (%)	51.5	63	Richland WA	−7	Bradenton FL
In-migrant hh.					
1980 (%)	18.9	44	Temple TX	5	Paterson NJ Saginaw MI
1990 (%)	18.0	39	Temple TX	6	Johnstown PA
change (%)[e]	−0.5	100	Saginaw MI	−40	Richland WA
Persons per hh.					
1980	2.73	4.7	McAllen TX	2.4	Charleston SC
1990	2.08	3.7	McAllen TX	2.2	Sarasota FL
change (%)	−14.6	20	Dallas TX	−25	Pittsburgh PA
Skill[a]					
Median education (25–64 years old)					
1980 (yr.)	14.1	16	Tallahassee FL Ann Arbor MI Washington DC	12	McAllen TX
1990 (yr.)	15.5	17	Ann Arbor MI	14	McAllen TX
change (%)	10.1	25	Brownsville TX	0	Washington DC
Education Gini					
1980	0.103	0.23	McAllen TX	0.08	Lima OH Janesville WI
1990	0.128	0.24	McAllen TX	0.10	Fayetteville NC
change (%)	25	50	Lawrence MA	−1	Stockton CA

Table 3.3 (continued)

Characteristics	Mean	Standard deviation	Highest value		Lowest value	
Labor market[a]						
Earnings Gini						
1979	0.454	0.020	0.535	Provo UT	0.398	Fall River MA
1989	0.466	0.022	0.537	Provo UT	0.382	Waterbury CT
change (%)	2.8	3.3	10	Pittsburgh PA	−9	Bridgeport CT
Employment/pop. ratio (25–64 yrs.)						
1980	0.699	0.042	0.79	MadisonWI	0.55	Johnstown PA
1990	0.747	0.045	0.85	Madison WI	0.59	McAllen TX
change (%)	6.9	4.1	18	Stockton CA	−5	McAllen TX
Other						
Workers in central city[e]						
1980 (%)	56.5	16.6	96	Lincoln NB	18	Benton Harbor MI
1990 (%)	55.1	17.9	94	El Paso TX	12	Benton Harbor MI
change (%)	−2.4	15.5	49.8	Fort Collins CO	−49.0	Charleston SC
Residents in central city						
1980 (%)	40.7	15.3	89	El Paso TX	13	Benton Harbor MI
1990 (%)	41.0	18.0	89	Lincoln NB	12	Benton Harbor MI
change (%)	−5.2	7.5	17	Chico CA	−28	Atlanta GA

			Maximum	Minimum
Change in ratio of % workers/ % residents in central city (%)	3.15	15.5	53.8 South Bend IN	−44.3 Charleston SC
Population[e] (000)				
1980	812.1	1142.3	8275 New York NY	139 Janesville WI
1990	898.6	1249.3	8863 Los Angeles CA	132 Alexandria LA
change (%)	13.1	14.8	66.2 Riverside CA	−11.3 Fall River MA
Per capita income[a]				
1979 ($)	7184	780	10210 Stamford CT	4006 McAllen TX
1989 ($)	13906	2523	26402 Stamford CT	6410 McAllen TX
change (%)	93	19.0	158 Stamford CT	50 Richland WA
Residential segregation index[f]				
1980	69.1	11.6	91.0 Bradenton FL	38 Lawrence MA
1990	65.1	11.4	91.0 Fort Wayne IN	40 Santa Cruz CA
change (%)	−5.8	5.3	7.9 Lawrence MA	−21 Melbourne FL

[a] Compiled by author from the 1980 and 1990 U.S. censuses 5% Public Use Micro Samples (PUMS).

[b] hh. = household(s).

[c] The "change" rows are computed by taking the mean of the change rates for all MSAs in the study. The MSA change rate is computed by subtracting the 1980 mean from the 1990 mean and dividing the difference by the 1980 mean.

[d] Elderly = over age 65.

[e] U.S. Bureau of the Census (1982, 1992).

[f] As compiled and reported by Farley and Frey (1993).

growth in per capita income among the 182 MSAs between 1979 and 1989.

There were substantial decreases in the size of the typical household, from an average of 2.73 persons in 1980 to 2.08 in 1990: in McAllen (which had the largest households among the MSAs), the average household lost a person, dropping from 4.7 to 3.7 persons. Although a handful of MSAs had increases in family size (including Dallas, in which the average size increased by 20 percent), most had decreases in size, with an average of –14.6 percent. These decreases in household size arise from the increase in one-person households and also are associated with the age, race, and gender composition of households.

The change in household size may have profound effects (as discussed in Chapter 2) on the distribution of income and on poverty rates. Because the distribution of household income and the poverty rate are measured for the households in which income earners reside, these measures may change when the income earners redistribute themselves across households, even if the income flow to individual earners is unchanged. For example, when couples divorce, a middle-income household may be transformed into two low-income households or one high-income and one low-income household. When young adults leave home, a high- or middle-income household may be transformed into two high- or middle-income households.

The average MSA had an increase in the proportion of its households that were headed by women and also in those including African Americans. In the average MSA, 32 percent of households were headed by women in 1990, up from 28 percent in 1980; the average MSA experienced a 15.3 percent increase in the proportion of its households headed by women. The average African-American proportion of the population increased from 9.2 percent to 11.0 percent, with the average MSA increasing its African-American representation by 27.9 percent. Jackson, Mississippi, has the highest African-American proportion of households, and Provo, Utah, the lowest. The households headed by persons over age 65 increased from a mean of 7.6 percent to 11.7 percent, with the average metropolis experiencing an increase of over 50 percent. Two Florida MSAs had the highest proportions over age 65 in 1980 and 1990, while Fayetteville, North Carolina, had the lowest proportion in 1990.

Although the ratio of employment to population between the ages of 25 and 64 increased, Table 3.3 shows that the increase was not evenly distributed across households. The proportion of households with no earners increased, with the growth in employment flowing entirely to households with multiple earners. The average MSA experienced an increase of 7.3 percent in the proportion of in-migrants in the population, although the mean proportion was 15 percent in both 1980 and 1990. This can be the case because MSAs with smaller proportions of in-migrants in 1980 tended to have greater percentage increases in that proportion, and MSAs with larger proportions in 1980 tended to have smaller percentage decreases. Households with multiple earners increased from 52 percent to 54 percent of households in the average MSA, and the average MSA experienced an increase of 6.9 percent in this proportion. Therefore, the effects of increases in the employment-to-population ratio on household income inequality or on the incidence of poverty (which is a household income measure) were mediated by the household formation decisions of employed persons.

Demographic Relationships

Among the MSAs shown in Figures 3.2a–c, there is substantial variation in both the levels of and the rates of change in household size, the proportion of the population who inmigrated to the MSA in the last five years, and the racial, gender, and age composition of households (Table 3.4). While there is no obvious pattern in household size among the MSAs of group A, the MSAs in groups B and C that did not have a two-digit decrease in household size were those with the least increase in household income inequality (New York City, Philadelphia, Lawrence, and Lincoln). There appears to be a strong relationship between changes in the proportion of households headed only by women and changes in household income inequality. For all three groups, the MSA with the greatest increase in female household heads also had the greatest increase in household income inequality (Chicago, Pittsburgh, and Lowell); for groups B and C, the MSAs with the least increase in female household heads also had the least increase in household income inequality (Philadelphia and Lincoln).

Other characteristics showed less obvious patterns. Although for all three groups, the MSA with the greatest increase in the proportion of households headed by a person over age 65 had the greatest increase in household income inequality (Chicago, Pittsburgh, and Lowell), there is no relationship between changes in age composition and changes in household income inequality for the remaining MSAs. Changes in the proportion of African Americans and in the proportion of residents who had moved into the MSA in the last five years also showed little connection to changes in household income inequality.

Table 3.4 also illustrates the connections between the race, gender, and age compositions of households in MSAs. MSAs with larger proportions of female heads of household usually have larger proportions of either elderly heads of households or African Americans. New York City has the largest proportion of female household heads on the list and also has among the highest proportions of both elderly and African-American households. Los Angeles had the slowest growth in female householders of the MSAs on Table 3.4 and also had among the lowest growth rates for both elderly and African-American householders.

Skill Composition

The skill composition of metropolitan residents may also affect the equality of earnings distribution and household income distribution and the amount of poverty in the MSA. To the extent that inequality in educational attainment arises from a larger proportion of the population having low levels of education, there is increased competition among workers for less-skilled jobs, resulting in relatively lower earnings and higher poverty rates. A shortage of persons with higher levels

Table 3.4 Demographic Characteristics of Selected MSAs

MSAs[a]	Household size 1990	Household size Change since 1980 (%)	Female household head 1990 (%)	Female household head Change since 1980 (%)	Elderly household head 1990 (%)	Elderly household head Change since 1980 (%)	African Americans 1990 (% of pop.)	African Americans Change since 1980 (%)	In-migrants 1990 (%)	In-migrants Change since 1980 (%)
Group A										
Chicago	2.73	−2.9	34.7	15.7	20.4	26.7	12.9	−6.3	26.5	−4.1
Los Angeles	2.97	10.4	33.0	4.5	17.3	11.4	9.8	−22.7	14.6	−1.7
Dallas	3.27	20.3	29.5	11.3	13.4	−0.4	10.4	−26.2	16.3	0.1
San Diego	2.73	4.0	30.8	8.9	18.8	14.7	5.7	3.1	56.1	−12.6
Norfolk	2.64	−5.1	26.3	7.8	18.6	18.7	29.3	5.5	22.0	51.6
Group B										
Pittsburgh	2.47	−25.1	33.8	19.7	27.4	27.6	6.8	21.5	30.0	0.8
Buffalo	2.55	−24.2	35.2	15.8	24.2	19.2	8.9	36.8	18.3	15.5
Newark	2.78	−20.9	34.1	9.3	21.7	22.8	21.5	37.5	12.7	6.6
Johnstown	2.61	−25.0	28.5	11.0	29.2	17.6	1.0	−33.9	5.7	1.7
New York City	2.63	2.8	43.2	11.3	22.5	11.0	22.8	5.7	14.1	7.1
Philadelphia	2.72	−3.3	32.8	4.8	21.9	15.0	14.8	−21.5	15.7	15.7

(continued)

Table 3.4 (continued)

MSAs[a]	Household size 1990	Household size Change since 1980 (%)	Female household head 1990 (%)	Female household head Change since 1980 (%)	Elderly household head 1990 (%)	Elderly household head Change since 1980 (%)	African Americans 1990 (% of pop.)	African Americans Change since 1980 (%)	In-migrants 1990 (%)	In-migrants Change since 1980 (%)
Group C										
Lowell	2.89	-12.7	32.0	76.0	16.6	63.5	1.2	101.3	8.7	38.3
Lafayette	2.71	-24.7	29.7	26.4	14.6	31.7	20.4	38.4	15.7	-21.4
Raleigh	2.49	-22.7	33.9	12.1	13.8	6.6	25.0	32.4	43.6	16.2
Lawrence	2.76	4.4	42.7	20.7	22.9	-2.9	4.5	207.9	18.3	21.4
Lincoln	2.52	0.1	30.7	6.3	17.7	10.2	1.7	-3.7	20.5	-6.9

[a] Listed within groups by percentage change in household income Gini, highest to lowest.

of education increases their already-higher wages, increasing inequality.

The median education of adults aged 25 to 64 increased from 14.1 to 15.5 years in the average MSA, with an average increase of 10.1 percent between 1980 and 1990 (see Table 3.3).[4] The distribution of education became more unequal, however, as shown by the Gini coefficient measuring the distribution of highest year of education attained: the Gini across the adult population in MSAs increased from 0.103 to 0.128. McAllen, Texas, had both the lowest median education and the most unequal distribution of education of all MSAs in both 1980 and 1990. The average increase in MSA educational inequality was 25 percent, a very large rate of growth, especially in the context of the changes in income and earnings Ginis reported in Table 3.1 (even though the base for the educational Gini is smaller, allowing a change to have a greater "growth" effect).

Education Relationships

For the selected MSAs, Table 3.5 shows how education and its distribution changed among wage earners between the ages of 25 and 64. Table 3.5 reports the proportion of the earners who had attained between 12 and 16 years of education and the educational Gini. The "least educated"[5] MSAs are Los Angeles, New York City, and Lawrence; the "best educated" are Lincoln ("college town" and state capital), Norfolk (naval base), Johnstown, and Pittsburgh.

The MSAs with lower educational attainment also had more educational inequality. Los Angeles and New York City have the greatest inequality and the lowest education; Lawrence is next on both dimensions. Lincoln has the highest education and the least inequality.

The changes over the decade show a similar relationship across the columns. MSAs that had greater rates of increase in the proportion of earners with 12 to 16 years of education tend to have less increase in educational inequality. The greatest increases in the proportion of earners with 12 to 16 years of education were for Norfolk and Lafayette; both had relatively modest increases in their education Ginis. Lowell, Lawrence, and Los Angeles showed modest increases in the proportion of earners with 12 to 16 years of education, and their increases in the educational Gini were relatively high. However, these education data do not clearly distinguish patterns that differentiate those MSAs that had less income divergence, or income divergence seemingly out of line with earnings divergence, from the others.

Local Labor Market

As the primary source of income for most households, both the quantity and the quality of jobs available in the local labor market are likely to influence household income inequality and poverty levels. The distribution of the quality of jobs (at least in terms of their wages) is represented by the Gini coefficient for wage and salary income across all earners in the MSA. Greater earnings inequality is expected to create more poverty in the MSA.[6] Measures of the availability (quantity) of jobs must be sensitive to the overall competition for the jobs. The availability of jobs is measured by the ratio of employment to the 25- to 64-year-old population in the MSA. As this proportion increases, workers in the MSA find it easier to find a job and the labor market is tighter. Increasing tightness of the labor market raises all wages, but particularly the wages of less-skilled workers relative to high-skilled workers, which reduces poverty.

The data in Table 3.3 indicate that there was an increase in earnings inequality within MSAs, leading to the expectation that poverty would increase. The average Gini coefficient for wage and salary income increased from 0.454 in 1979 to 0.466. The average MSA had an increase of 2.8 percent in its Gini coefficient for earnings. Counteracting this upwards pressure on poverty rates was the fact that the ratio of employment to population between ages 25 and 64 increased from an average of 69.9 percent to 74.7 percent, with the growth in this proportion averaging 6.9 percent between 1980 and 1990. Madison, Wisconsin, had the highest ratio in 1980 and 1990, while McAllen, Texas, had the lowest in 1990 and also had the greatest decrease in this ratio between 1980 and 1990.

Table 3.5 Skill Characteristics of Selected MSAs

MSAs[a]	Earners with 12–16 years of education		Education Gini	
	1990 (%)	Change since 1980 (%)	1990	Change since 1980 (%)
Group A				
Chicago	76.7	11.9	0.136	23.1
Los Angeles	71.4	5.2	0.171	35.4
Dallas	77.0	12.9	0.138	26.5
San Diego	80.7	8.4	0.126	26.8
Norfolk	82.0	15.4	0.113	15.2
Group B				
Pittsburgh	82.0	8.9	0.114	25.9
Buffalo	79.9	10.9	0.120	24.1
Newark	75.3	9.4	0.138	21.7
Johnstown	82.0	7.9	0.104	24.2
New York City	72.3	11.9	0.152	20.3
Philadelphia	78.6	11.2	0.125	33.9
Group C				
Lowell	77.8	2.4	0.130	44.8
Lafayette	79.0	15.3	0.131	8.7
Raleigh	77.6	13.3	0.126	13.8
Lawrence	73.8	7.2	0.151	50.1
Lincoln	83.6	9.6	0.107	17.4

[a] Listed within groups by percentage change in household income Gini, highest to lowest.

Employment Relationships

In the groups of selected MSAs, four—Norfolk, Lowell, Raleigh, and Lincoln—moved toward greater equality in the earnings distribution among workers (Table 3.6). Norfolk, Lincoln, and Raleigh also had strong increases in job availability (employment-to-population ratio), while Lowell had a smaller increase. Consistent with the observation made by Freeman (1996) about institutionally set wages being more equally distributed (discussed in Chapter 2), Norfolk, Raleigh, and Lincoln are centers for government employment.

For Norfolk, the employment increase translated into a large decrease in the proportion of households without earners, but Lowell, Raleigh, and Lincoln all saw their proportion of households without earners increase. Because these three MSAs had relatively low proportions of households without earners (10 or 11 percent in 1989), the increase was on a very small base. Nonetheless, these data point to the importance of the number of jobs and their distribution among households in mediating the effects of shifts in the wage distribution.

If an MSA's population is aging, then there may be an increase in the proportion of elderly households that include retired workers and, therefore, an increase in no-earner households. This appears to have been the case for Lowell and Lafayette, for example; Lowell had a 63.5 percent increase and Lafayette a 31.7 percent increase in the proportion of householders that were over age 65 (see Table 3.4). A similar pattern exists for Pittsburgh.

Employment-to-population ratios decreased in only Lafayette and Lawrence. These two MSAs have the lowest employment-to-population ratios in the small MSA group, at 0.70.

Given that within each group, the MSAs are listed in order of their 1979–1989 change in household income inequality (greatest to least), both the employment-to-population ratio and the proportion of no-earner households appear related to household income inequality. Those MSAs listed first in each group (Table 3.6) generally have lower rates of growth in employment-to-population ratio and higher rates of growth in no-earner households. The growth in no-earner households might be more important, however. New York City experienced relatively less growth in household income inequality and had little change in the employment-to-population ratio; there was a substantial decrease, however, in no-earner households. Lowell and Lawrence, Massachusetts, also provide interesting cases. Lowell had a greater rate of increase in household income inequality, even though it had a slight increase in the employment ratio and Lawrence had a decrease. Yet, there is a substantial difference between these two small Massachusetts MSAs in the rate at which the proportion of no-earner households grew.

While the data on the local labor market from these selected MSAs are consistent with labor markets strongly influencing household income inequality, it is very clear that the distribution of employment across households may also be an important consideration. The way that earners form households or that household members decide about seeking jobs may counteract or expand the influence of local labor market changes.

Structural Characteristics

The geography of an MSA may affect the level of income inequality or of poverty and its distribution between city and suburbs. MSAs with more population growth are experiencing greater rates of economic growth, resulting in lower poverty levels. MSAs that are becoming more politically and economically integrated (as represented by slower decreases in the proportion of the metropolitan population living in the central city, annexation of surrounding communities by the central city, and less residential segregation by race) are expected to have less poverty and income inequality.

Table 3.3 indicates that the average MSA population in the sample in 1990 was 898,600, with Los Angeles the largest and Alexandria, Louisiana, the smallest of the 182 MSAs. The greatest population

Table 3.6 Local Labor Market Conditions in Selected MSAs

MSAs[a]	Earnings Gini		Employment/pop. ratio		No-earner hh.	
	1989	Change since 1979 (%)	1989	Change since 1979 (%)	1989 (%)	Change since 1979 (%)
Group A						
Chicago	0.462	5.9	0.76	5.8	14	4.2
Los Angeles	0.483	6.5	0.73	2.5	14	-0.4
Dallas	0.474	5.5	0.79	2.8	16	-0.1
San Diego	0.469	0.7	0.76	8.8	17	-9.2
Norfolk	0.438	-0.9	0.77	10.3	11	-11.0
Group B						
Pittsburgh	0.485	10.1	0.70	9.4	20	20.3
Buffalo	0.467	4.2	0.72	9.7	17	10.6
Newark	0.474	4.0	0.77	7.4	12	-12.1
Johnstown	0.451	0.6	0.65	17.3	23	12.5
New York City	0.463	6.1	0.70	3.7	18	-16.0
Philadelphia	0.461	2.8	0.76	12.4	15	-13.5
Group C						
Lowell	0.425	-2.3	0.77	1.4	10	48.7
Lafayette	0.497	2.6	0.70	-1.7	16	45.9
Raleigh	0.456	-0.9	0.82	5.6	10	1.6
Lawrence	0.397	0.7	0.70	-3.5	20	16.8
Lincoln	0.468	-0.4	0.84	6.0	11	18.2

[a] Listed within groups by percentage change in household income Gini, highest to lowest.

growth (66.2 percent) was experienced by Riverside, California, and the least by Fall River, Massachusetts (–11.3 percent). The proportion of the metropolitan workforce employed in the central city averaged 0.565 in 1980, decreasing to 0.551 in 1990; El Paso, Texas, had the highest proportion in 1990 and Benton Harbor, Michigan, had the lowest in both years. The average MSA experienced a decrease of 2.4 percent in this proportion; Fort Collins, Colorado (which engaged in substantial annexation), experienced the greatest percentage increase and Charleston, South Carolina, the greatest decrease. A smaller proportion of MSA residents live in the central city, about 0.410 in both years. Because the average central city's proportion of MSA residents decreased more than its proportion of workers, the average MSA increased the workers/residents ratio in the central city by 3.15 percent (Table 3.3).

Annexation of surrounding communities by the central city was common (data not shown) with the average MSA central city increasing its physical territory by 13 percent; a handful of central cities ceded small areas to other communities.

African Americans residing in these MSAs became less residentially segregated over the decade. The greatest increase in segregation index was for Lawrence, Massachusetts, which has one of the lowest absolute levels of segregation in the nation; Melbourne, Florida, had the greatest decline.

Population Relationships

For the selected MSAs, Table 3.7 shows that, at least for groups A and B, the MSAs with the greatest growth in household income inequality tended to be losing population. This was true for Chicago, Pittsburgh, Buffalo, Newark, and Johnstown. The MSAs with the least growth in inequality also seemed to be growing in population, as was the case for Dallas, San Diego, Norfolk, Raleigh, and Lawrence.

Most central cities lost population share to their surrounding suburbs, while their share of the MSA's poor population increased (see Figure 1.3). Other than New York City (which experienced slight growth), the central cities of the larger MSAs declined in MSA population share. There was no apparent relationship between changes in household income inequality and changes in the proportion of MSA residents in the central city.

There was more variation in the ratio of the central city's proportion of MSA jobs to its proportion of the MSA residents. The central cities of Pittsburgh and New York City decreased in this ratio, indicating that the job market may have become more difficult for central city residents. Improvement in the central city job market appears to have little relationship to changes in household income inequality among these MSAs.

Racial segregation declined in these MSAs. The MSAs with the least growth in household inequality (all MSAs in group A) had larger decreases in segregation; however, there is no other apparent relationship for the MSAs in Table 3.7 between rates of change in racial segregation and in household income inequality.

SUMMARY

There are substantial variations in earnings and income inequality; poverty rates; demographic and skill compositions; geographic structure; and labor market opportunities among MSAs. While for some of the MSAs highlighted in this chapter, household income inequality and earnings inequality have changed in similar ways, for others there are very dramatic differences. Some of these MSAs have experienced changes in household structure and in the distribution of employment that may plausibly explain why changes in earnings inequality did not translate directly into changes in household inequality.

A more systematic exploration of variations in these characteristics across MSAs provides a potential means for identifying the characteristics of local economies that are associated with growth in income inequality and poverty rates and with differential growth in the concentration of poverty in central cities.

Table 3.7 MSA Structure, Selected MSAs

MSAs[a]	Central city annexation (%)	Change in population since 1980 (%)	Proportion residents in central city 1990 (%)	Change since 1980 (%)	Change since 1980 in jobs/residents ratio in central city (%)	Black/white segregation index 1990	Change since 1980 (%)
Group A							
Chicago	0.2	−7.4	48.1	−6.8	4.0	87	−4.4
Los Angeles	0.9	18.5	48.2	−0.6	9.7	71	−11.3
Dallas	10.7	30.6	55.0	−9.3	14.7	66	−18.5
San Diego	3.4	34.2	48.8	−3.5	4.7	59	−6.3
Norfolk	0.4	20.3	81.8	−2.5	−3.7	57	−12.3
Group B							
Pittsburgh	0.0	−7.3	19.3	−6.1	−27.0	75	0.0
Buffalo	0.0	−4.3	35.3	−4.0	15.3	84	0.0
Newark	0.0	−7.2	23.2	−8.8	34.7	83	−1.2
Johnstown	3.5	−9.1	13.2	−12.0	−18.1	82	0.0
New York City	0.0	3.3	86.2	0.2	−7.6	78	0.0
Philadelphia	0.0	3.0	38.3	−8.5	1.6	82	−1.2

(continued)

Table 3.7 (continued)

MSAs[a]	Central city annexation (%)	Change in population since 1980 (%)	Proportion residents in central city		Change since 1980 in jobs/residents ratio in central city (%)	Black/white segregation index	
			1990 (%)	Change since 1980 (%)		1990	Change since 1980 (%)
Group C							
Lowell	7.0	17.2	39.5	–4.5	–12.1	65	–5.9
Lafayette	51.3	10.0	47.4	–5.1	–5.2	60	–3.2
Raleigh	66.7	31.6	54.2	–11.4	–11.4	57	–8.1
Lawrence	4.5	39.7	39.0	–20.6	–12.4	41	7.9
Lincoln	5.5	10.9	89.1	0.7	–0.9	49	–3.9

[a] Listed within groups by percentage change in household income Gini, highest to lowest.

Notes

1. The 182 largest MSAs in this study are those MSAs included in the 200 largest by population size in both 1980 and 1990. A complete list of these MSAs and the data used in the analyses appear in the Appendix.

2. The Gini coefficient measures the difference between the actual distribution and a completely equal distribution of income or earnings. It takes on values between 0 and 1. If, in actuality, all MSA residents had the same income or wage levels, then there would be no difference between the actual distribution and a completely equal distribution. The Gini coefficient would be 0. At the other extreme, if all income were received by only one household and the others had no income, the Gini coefficient would be 1. The Gini coefficient is discussed in greater detail in the next chapter.

3. In 1990, 2 percent of the residents who were in-migrants came from abroad or from nonmetropolitan U.S. locations.

4. There was a change in the way that educational attainment was reported between the 1980 and the 1990 censuses. The 1980 census reported by year of final attainment, while the 1990 census aggregated across some years (such as grades 1 to 4 and 5 to 8) and reported type of education rather than years for those with 13 to 15 years). For 1990, the median value for the aggregated category was assigned to each individual in the category and a similar "aggregation" and assignment of median value was done for 1980. Fewer than 1 percent of persons age 25 to 64 in 1990 were in the aggregated categories for the lower levels of education.

5. Assuming that persons who did not fall between 12 and 16 years of education were more likely to be high school drop-outs than graduate-school attendees.

6. Poverty rates are defined with respect to *household* income and size. It is important to distinguish the earnings Gini, which results from the labor market conditions facing individual workers, from household income inequality and household or personal poverty rates, which result from the household formation decisions of income producers, as well as from the earnings inequality among those producers.

4 Measuring Effects of MSA Characteristics on Income Distribution

The data in Chapter 3 document the wide range of experiences in both the levels of inequality and poverty among U.S. metropolitan areas and the different changes in those measures during the 1980s. Can we get a better understanding of why metropolitan area experiences are different? This chapter discusses several methodological issues raised by an analysis of the experiences of metropolitan areas, including issues involved in 1) measurement of income distribution; 2) geographic boundaries for measuring income distributional differences; 3) methods for analyzing how demographic factors influence aggregate measures of distribution; and 4) the models and specifications used to estimate the correlates of changes in this study.

MEASURING INCOME DISTRIBUTION

The discussion of potential causes and effects of changes in the income distribution or of policies to alter the income distribution must be premised on measurements of the relative equality of the distribution.

How Income Is Measured

Current income is the sum of monetary wages and salaries, net income from self-employment, Social Security income plus cash transfers from other government programs, property income (for example, interests, dividends, net rental income), and other forms of cash income (such as private pensions and alimony). Current income does not include capital gains, imputed rents from owner-occupied housing, or government or private benefits in-kind (such as food stamps, Medicare benefits, employer-provided health insurance or other fringe benefits), nor does it subtract taxes (although all of these affect a household's or an individual's consumption levels).

Novak and Green (1986) argued that the patterns of increasing household inequality and poverty rates are far overstated because of the increasing importance of in-kind government benefits (such as health care, food stamps, and public housing) and of fringe benefits in the compensation package that workers receive. They report that food, housing, and medical noncash assistance targeted to low-income persons totals more than twice the amount distributed as cash assistance.

Noncash assistance programs were initiated in the late 1960s and early 1970s and were then expanded. There is little evidence that these in-kind government benefits compensate, however, for the increasing inequality documented for the 1980s. The proportion of households receiving noncash benefits (including food stamps, school lunches, public housing, and/or Medicaid) actually declined from 17.3 percent of U.S. households in 1980 to 16.1 percent in 1989.[1] In addition, the value of the benefits received per household declined in real terms.

Novak and Green also reported that employer contributions for employee pension and health benefits are three times the level of government noncash assistance targeted to low-income families. Because these payments are more likely to flow to middle- and upper-income families, however, they may actually increase income inequality. Smeeding (1983) reported that the addition of fringe benefits to earnings increased the Gini coefficient for all earners by 3.1 points.

Computations of income equality that include noncash income are not likely to show less growth in inequality. In fact, Cutler and Katz (1992) analyzed consumption (as opposed to income) data and found strong evidence of increasing household inequality.

The analyses presented in this book are based entirely on cash income reported by respondents to the U.S. census. Because these respondents do not report on fringe benefits or other non-monetary sources of income, I am not able to include such income. While those who have examined these items in more detail in the national economy have found that their inclusion does not substantially alter the measured changes in equality based on money income, I do not know how the inclusion of this income would alter the way that inequality changed across MSAs in the 1980s.

How Inequality Is Measured

The most commonly used measure of income inequality in the popular media is the poverty rate, which provides a measure of the proportion of persons whose income is not sufficient to provide for a defined set of basic needs. It is also possible to examine the share of total income accruing to various segments of the income distribution, such as the proportion of total income accruing to each quintile. Studies of earnings or income inequality, however, typically rely on a scalar measure of income inequality that permits comparisons between the relative equality of alternative distributions. A typical measure, such as the Gini coefficient, ranks a set of distributions in terms of increasing inequality. It is well known, however, that the Gini coefficient does not necessarily rank a given set of distributions in the same way as other measures (such as the coefficient of variation or the variance of the natural log of earnings or income [Sen 1973; Slottje 1989; Karoly 1988, 1992]). The poverty rate and the Gini coefficient, used in this study, are explored in more detail below.

Poverty Rate

Persons or households are considered to be poor, or in poverty, if their incomes are below the poverty level defined by a threshold developed by the U.S. Social Security Administration in 1963. The index is based solely on money income and does not reflect the fact that many low-income persons receive noncash benefits. Income thresholds are defined separately by family size and the age of the household head, in each case based on the 1963 cost of an inexpensive, but nutritionally sound, food plan designed by the U.S. Department of Agriculture. This cost is multiplied by three (assuming that households spend one-third of their income on food) and has been adjusted upward by changes in the Consumer Price Index since 1963. For a household of four persons, the 1989 poverty-level income was $12,675, based on inflationary adjustments to the 1963 level of $3,128; for a one-person household, under age 65, the 1989 poverty-level income was $6,311. There is an equivalence scaling implicit in the poverty rate that reduces the necessary per capita income as household size increases.

Gini Coefficient

The Gini coefficient, a widely used distributional index that takes on values between 0 and 1, measures the difference between the actual distribution and a completely equal distribution of income or earnings. If, in actuality, all incomes were the same, then there would be no difference between the actual distribution and a completely equal distribution, and the Gini coefficient would be 0. At the other extreme, if all income was received by only one household, the Gini coefficient would be 1. Unlike the poverty rate, the Gini coefficient does not take account of household size; i.e., there is no equivalence scaling that adjusts for well-being based on household size.

The U.S. census tabulates and publishes Gini coefficients only for the family distribution of income. A family is defined as a group of two or more persons related by birth, marriage, or adoption and residing in the same household. A household is defined as the person or the group of persons that occupies a housing unit. Individuals living alone or with unrelated individuals are not counted as families. Because the proportion of the population living in families has declined, changes in the family Gini coefficient over time (or spatial areas) may arise from changes in who lives in families as well as changes in how income flows to families. The Gini coefficient for household income, which includes the entire non-institutionalized population, is not subject to this selection bias.

Although the Gini coefficient is a commonly used index of inequality, it is harder to interpret than the poverty rate or shares of income accruing to persons in various proportions of the distribution. The Gini coefficient is more sensitive to changes in the middle of the distribution than it is to changes at the extreme ends. It also does not distinguish between inequality caused by very high incomes in the upper levels of the distribution and that caused by very low incomes at the extreme bottom.

Many studies that report Gini coefficients use calculations based on grouped data, frequently computed for the earnings and income data reported by the U.S. Census Bureau in Current Population Reports, Consumer Income, Series P-60.[2] Gini coefficients computed from grouped data tend to be lower than those computed from individual data because of the "smooth-out" differences within quintiles or deciles.

In order to evaluate overall changes in income equality, to consider the effect of income on well-being, and to examine which segments of the income distribution account for changes, this study will analyze the poverty rate for individuals, the household Gini coefficient,[3] and the shares accruing to quintiles of households.

UNITS OF ANALYSIS: RATES OF CHANGE WITHIN MSA BOUNDARIES

An analysis that attempts to measure the factors that contribute to changes in the distribution of income must be a macro, or an economy-wide, analysis. The distribution of income is, by definition, a measure that aggregates the experiences of individuals, households, etc., in a particular economy. While data on individuals can be used to analyze the determinants of *individual levels* of earnings or of decisions to form households, the measurement of income distribution differences requires information on how individuals rank vis-a-vis other individuals in the economy, and also on the magnitude of the differences in income or wages between any two ranks. These measures can only be derived in the context of an entire economy.

Subnational areas, for which market exchanges are substantially greater among areas within the boundaries than they are among areas outside the boundaries, constitute markets and, in that sense, economies. To the extent that there are several subnational areas that can be delineated as markets or economies, we have "more data" that can be used to analyzed the relationship between the characteristics of the economy or the market and inequality. As explained in the first chapter, metropolitan areas are defined by such exchanges and constitute economies. Although the nation also represents an economy "for which market exchanges are substantially greater among areas within the boundaries than they are among areas outside the boundaries," inequality within the local market is also of direct policy concern: residents may be more sensitive to local inequality and local area markets have a substantial influence upon income of residents.

Cross-sectional studies of areas such as MSAs raise a different set of difficulties, however.[4] There are likely to be many more underlying differences between any two metropolitan areas at the same point in time than there are between two time periods within the same metropolitan area or nation. Many, probably most, of these differences are not easily measured. These differences may be correlated with some of the measured characteristics that are of prime policy or analytical interest. For example, consider the case of MSAs dominated by a large research university—such as Urbana, Illinois, or Gainesville, Florida. These MSAs have different educational, migration, and labor force participation characteristics and a different age distribution than other MSAs of similar size and regional location. They also have a disproportionate share of households and earners with relatively low income for their educational attainment. These incomes are low because household members, often working at least part time, are pursuing a degree or supporting a family member in his or her pursuit of a degree. Their incomes will rise later, but, for most, at a different location. A study that examined the effects of labor force participation, education, and migration on poverty rates or income inequality in these MSAs, without taking note of the unique situation, would underestimate the effect of education and labor force participation by the more educated on income and poverty. It would be misleading. While these particular unique characteristics could be measured, they are illustrative of the types of differences that exist in MSAs that make cross-sectional comparisons problematic. Other MSAs may offer an amenity that appeal to a particular class of workers or households and result in their willingness to take lower earnings. It is difficult to measure these subtleties in a large cross-sectional analysis.

MSAs offer a large number of observations of different markets that permit a statistical analysis of the correlates of and effects of various characteristics on income inequality and poverty, but, any such study must develop a methodology that considers the "unobserved" differences between MSAs that are correlated with the study variables. By comparing changes in the MSA income inequality over a decade, the effects of "unobserved" differences between MSAs that affect inequality but that do not change over the decade (i.e., fixed effects) can be eliminated.

In order to improve our understanding of how the characteristics of a macro-economy are related to inequality and poverty within the economy, this study examines changes in inequality and poverty within MSAs over a decade.

ANALYZING THE ROLE OF DEMOGRAPHICS

Inequality has been measured and analyzed for the distribution of income or wages among individuals, among households, and among spatial units such as census divisions or municipalities and census tracts in the same urban area. As wages accrue to individuals, it is reasonable to measure inequality in terms of differences among individuals. Indexes of wage or earnings equality do not necessarily translate into indexes of income or consumption inequality among individuals.

With the exception of some studies that have examined the effect of changes in the return on capital,[5] discussion about the distribution of income or earnings proceeds as if the two distributions and their determinants were the same. Although earnings account for most household income and variations in earnings account for much of the growing inequality in household income, the growing gap between the richest and the poorest of households involves more than changes in earnings rates (or changes in returns on capital). The patterns of changes in household income inequality and in earnings inequality illustrated in Figures 1.1, 1.2, and 3.2a–c make it very clear that earnings inequality cannot explain household income inequality. Because households with no workers account for an increasing share of the poorest households, any change in the real wages of low-wage workers has no direct effect on their share of income. Among richer households, there is an increasing likelihood of multiple earners. While the incomes of such households are affected by the wage rates of their earners, they are also strongly affected by the number of earners. Inequality in the distribution of household income is also affected, therefore, by marriage, divorce, and fertility decisions, as well as by the labor force participation decisions of household members.

How Changes in Demographic Structure Affect Distribution

While measuring the Gini coefficient for subpopulations can be of assistance in helping us to understand the sources of the overall MSA shifts in the income or earnings distribution, it is incorrect to conclude that changes in the relative representation of segments of the population that have more or less unequal distributions account for the overall changes. For example, the distributions of earnings among women, African-American workers, and Hispanic workers have become more unequal during the 1980s, and their representation in the total workforce has increased. But even if the overall distribution did not change, we still might observe increasing inequality among these subpopulations as opportunities for advancement became more available.

The role of shifts in demographics cannot be measured by a "decomposition analysis" that sums the effects of changes for each particular demographic subgroup. While a decomposition analysis can define the direct effects of demographic shifts, it cannot detect interactions. Shifts in the distribution for one subgroup may affect distributions among other demographic groups and a decomposition analysis cannot detect these interactions. For example, the increasing inequality among women, African-American, and Hispanic workers mentioned above may increase inequality among men and non-black Hispanics, who now encounter more competition for high wage jobs and therefore are increasingly likely to have the low wage jobs that were previously occupied by minorities and women.

The direct effect of demographic characteristics of the population on income or earnings inequality within metropolitan areas depends on two factors: 1) the mean income or earnings of those having the characteristic compared with others; and 2) the relative equality of the distribution of income or earnings of those with the characteristic compared to others. In analyzing changes in income inequality within MSAs, then, the changes in mean income of the subpopulation and in their level of income equality relative to the total population are the relevant data. If the mean, or the change in the mean, is substantially lower (higher) than that of the rest of the population and the distribution, or the change in the distribution, is the same, increases in the proportion with the characteristic will increase inequality; if the mean, or the change in the mean, is close to the rest of the population, but the distribution (or the change in the distribution) is more unequal, increases in the proportion with the characteristic will increase inequality; all other combinations—i.e., an equivalent mean and equivalent distribution or a substantially lower (higher) mean but greater equality of distribution—mean that increases in the proportion with the characteristic will have less effect on the equality of the distribution.

Table 4.1 provides the Gini coefficient (MSA average), the mean household income (average across the means for MSAs) for various subpopulations of households for 1979 and 1989, and the change since 1979.

Table 4.1 Mean Gini Coefficient and Income for MSA Subpopulations of Households

Population	Gini	Multiple of 1979 Gini	Income ($)	Multiple of 1979 income
1979				
Total	0.37	–	17,144	–
Female-headed hh.	0.44	–	11,874	–
No-earner hh.	0.57	–	8,503	–
Multi-earner hh.	0.27	–	26,764	–
African-American-headed hh.	0.43	–	14,465	–
Elderly-headed hh.	0.45	–	12,238	–
In-migrant hh.	0.38	–	18,986	–
1989				
Total	0.41	1.11	31,930	1.86
Female-headed hh.	0.45	1.02	23,891	2.01
No-earner hh.	0.56	0.98	16,772	1.97
Multi-earner hh.	0.31	1.15	49,938	1.87
African-American-headed hh.	0.44	1.02	25,715	1.78
Elderly-headed hh.	0.45	1.00	24,832	2.03
In-migrant hh.	0.41	1.08	37,015	1.95

The proportion of households that have no earners and the proportion that have more than one earner affect income inequality. Households with no earners have substantially higher within-group inequality (Gini coefficients of 0.57 and 0.56, substantially higher than the 0.37 and 0.41 observed for all households) and lower average income than other households. Because households with no earners have substantially lower incomes than those with earners, MSAs experiencing increases in the proportion of no-earner households should experience increasing income inequality. As the distribution of income among no-earner households became more equal both absolutely and relative to the overall population between 1979 and 1989, however, and as their average income grew more than that of all households, the effects on MSA inequality of changes in the proportion of no-earner households was dampened.

Households with more than one earner have higher incomes than other households, but the within-group income distribution is more equal than for other households. Because these two characteristics are potentially offsetting in their effects on overall MSA inequality, the effect of increases in the proportion of households with more than one earner on household income inequality is not clear.

Because African-American households have both lower incomes and slightly more unequally distributed incomes than other households, increases in the proportion of households headed by African Americans are expected to increase inequality. The slower growth in income inequality (1.02) dampens the effect, while the slower growth in average income (1.78) increases the effect.

Because senior citizens have lower average incomes and more within-group income inequality than other household categories, increases in the proportion of households headed by persons over age 65 are expected to increase inequality. The changes between 1979 and 1989 (no change in inequality and greater growth in average income) would dampen the effect of changes in the age composition of households on overall MSA inequality.

Because households headed by women have fewer potential earners than households headed by couples and have earners with lower potential earnings, on average, than households headed by men, they have lower incomes than other households. Table 4.1 also indicates that female-headed households have slightly greater within-group income

inequality than other households. Therefore, MSAs with larger proportions of women-headed households are expected to have more inequality in household income. The greater increase in average income and
the slower increase in inequality would dampen that effect, however.

Increases in the rate of in-migration can be a result of inequality or
a cause of inequality. If inequality has prompted a relatively higher
income group to migrate, then the new in-migration should decrease
inequality. If the in-migration is not in response to the level or the distribution of income in the MSA but is prompted by (or is reflective of)
other characteristics of the metropolitan area, then the in-migration
may increase or decrease inequality, depending on the extent to which
the distribution of income among in-migrants is more or less equal
than the distribution among existing residents. Table 4.1 shows that in-
migrants in 1979 had within-group inequality (0.38) and income
($18,986) levels similar to those for all households, but in 1989 their
income advantage increased (as a proportion of 1979 income, 1.95 for
in-migrants vs. 1.86 for all households).

THE ANALYTICAL APPROACH

The debate over the sources of rising poverty and inequality in
both income and earnings is not a conceptual debate. The conceptual
framework is clear; it is the relative (or empirical) importance of the
forces that affect income or earnings inequality that is debated.

The theory of earnings inequality is based on the theory of wage
determination. Wages are relatively higher for more highly paid workers than for lower-wage workers when there is relatively greater
demand for highly paid workers, when there is relatively less supply of
highly skilled workers, or when there is an institutional force that sets
wages less equally. MSA differences in demand for workers by skill
level are measured by industrial structure, which reflects differences
arising from different techniques of production as well as differences
in the product produced. MSA differences in supply are measured by
the level and distribution of skills in the labor force and the overall
employment-to-population ratio. Institutional forces that affect earnings equality include the presence or absence of unions, market imper-

fections, or discriminatory behavior that interferes with the market determination of wages.

The sources of household income inequality, and poverty that is based on household income measurement, include the factors that affect earnings inequality, but also include factors that affect the way wage earners form households and the decisions of household members on whether and how much to work. Household income is higher as the number of wage earners residing in the household increases. The overall relationship between household income distribution and the number of wage earners depends, however, on whether households with a relatively high-end wage earner are more or less likely than those with a relatively low-end wage earner to have additional household members in the workforce.

We attempt to sort out the relationship between household inequality and changes in local labor market conditions from that between household inequality and changes in demographic or social structure. I estimate two equations: an equation to measure the systematic relationships between changes in an MSA's economic and demographic characteristics and changes in its household income inequality or poverty rate, and an equation measuring the systematic relationships between changes in an MSA's economic characteristics and various measures of earnings inequality.

These equations are estimated across the 182 largest MSAs using the percentage change[6] in the Ginis and characteristics. Specifically,

$$\Delta HYGINI_j = \alpha_0 + \alpha_1 \Delta DEM_j + \alpha_2 \Delta SKILL_j$$
$$+ \alpha_3 \Delta LOC_j + \alpha_4 \Delta LM_j + \varepsilon_j$$

and

$$\Delta EARNGINI_{ji} = \alpha_0 + \alpha_1 \Delta DEM_j + \alpha_2 \Delta SKILL_j$$
$$+ \alpha_3 \Delta LOC_j + \alpha_4 \Delta LM_j + \alpha_5 \Delta IND_j + \varepsilon_{ji}$$

where

$\Delta HYGINI_j$ = the change in the Gini coefficient for household income, or the change in the personal poverty rate,

ΔDEM_j = a vector of metropolitan-specific variables reflecting changes in MSA demographic characteristics;

$\Delta SKILL_j$ = a vector of MSA-specific variables reflecting changes in the skills of the local labor force; ΔLOC_j is a vector of MSA-specific variables reflecting changes in economic and structural characteristics;

ΔLM_j = a vector of MSA-specific variables reflecting changes in the labor market, including the distribution of earnings and the employment-to-population ratio;

$\Delta EARNGINI_{ji}$ = the change in the Gini coefficient for wage and salaries among workers of group i in metropolitan area j;

ΔIND_j = a vector of changes in MSA-specific variables reflecting the industrial composition of employment; and

$\varepsilon_j, \varepsilon_{ji}$ = are error terms.

The variables included in ΔDEM_j are the change in mean number of persons per household, the change in the proportions of households headed by women and by persons over age 65, the change in proportions of the population who are African American and who have moved into the metropolitan area in the last five years, and the change in proportions of households that include multiple earners and that include no earners.

The variation in demographic characteristics across MSAs is substantial. Table 3.3 shows that, in the average MSA, there was an increase of over 50 percent in the proportion of households headed by someone over 65 and of 15.3 percent in the proportion of households headed by women. The average MSA increased its African-American representation by 27.9 percent.

The variables included in $\Delta SKILL_j$, the change in median education and the change in a Gini coefficient computed on the distribution of the highest level of educational attainment across persons over age 25 in each metropolitan area, measure the skill distribution. Increases in the average level of educational attainment are expected to increase productivity, and therefore average earnings, but to decrease inequality (after controlling for the Gini coefficient on educational attainment), because increases in education decrease the significance of a year's difference in attainment.   The greater the Gini coefficient for education, the greater the Gini coefficient for earnings; that is, the more inequality in the distribution of education across the population, the greater the inequality in earnings.   These variables are also demographic or social variables that influence the equality of income across households or families, in that they affect the potential for sorting persons of more or less equal earnings potential across households.   The greater the Gini coefficient for education, the more inequality in the distribution of education across the population, and the greater the possibility that selective "mating" will magnify inequality in household or family income.

The variables included in ΔLOC_j, measuring changes in metropolitan economic and structural characteristics, are changes in mean income, population size, and the ratio of the proportion of the workforce employed in the central city of the MSA to the proportion of the MSA's residents living in the central city.   Although there has been much discussion about the effects of the level or character of economic development on inequality, there is no conceptual reason to expect that economic development decreases inequality.   Previous studies have consistently found, however, that inequality levels decrease with income levels.   Therefore, it is expected that increases in mean income will have a negative effect on changes in the Gini coefficient.   Change in population size is an index that reflects the effects of growth, economies (or diseconomies) of scale, labor market competition, and the cost of living on the distribution of income or earnings.   On one hand, if increases in income decrease inequality, an increase in the cost of living (which occurs as population size increases) should increase inequality, *ceteris paribus*.   On the other hand, increases in economies of scale and in efficiency that arise from increases in competition (both positively correlated with population) should decrease inequality. Therefore, the effect of changes in population size on inequality is *a priori* indeterminant.

Ginis for MSAs in the same region may depend not only on aggregate conditions in that MSA, but also on conditions in neighboring MSAs.   A series of regional dummies was included, but only that for the South (actually South Central) was close to significant.   Although MSAs in the South have historically had more unequal income distributions, it is not apparent whether those historic conditions should affect changes in the 1980s. The proportion of the population resident in the central city of the MSA measures the extent of municipal government fragmentation. Because greater fragmentation of local governments is both a cause and an effect of spatial variation in income, decreases in the proportion living in the city represent increases in fragmentation that are expected to be associated with increased inequality and poverty. The ratio of the proportion of the workforce employed in the central city of the MSA to the proportion of the population resident in the central city measures the importance of job accessibility to the lower-income persons, who are more likely than higher-income persons to be residing in the central city. Because greater suburbanization of employment is both a cause and an effect of spatial variation in income, increases in this ratio are expected to decrease poverty and inequality.

The variables included in ΔLM_j are the changes in the employment-to-population ratio and $\Delta EARNGINI_j$. $\Delta EARNGINI_j$, which will be defined alternately for all wage and salary workers and for full-time, full-year workers in the MSA, allows a precise control for the effects of the earnings structure of the local labor market. Obviously, we expect that $\Delta EARNGINI_j$ has a positive influence on changes in the inequality of household income, but the more important question is the relative importance of household formation patterns versus the effect of the earnings structure of the local labor market on household income inequality.

The variables included in ΔIND_j are measures of changes in industrial composition. The effects of industrial composition on earnings inequality depend on both the relationship of the mean wage in the industry to the mean wage in the region and the relationship of the distribution of wages within the industry to that within other industries in the region. Because durable-goods manufacturing pays a higher wage (but a more equally distributed wage) than other industries, MSAs experiencing an increase in the proportion of workers employed in durable-goods manufacturing are expected to experience a decrease in earnings inequality. Because producer services pay a higher but more unequally distributed wage than other industries, MSAs experiencing an increase in the proportion of workers employed in producer services are expected to experience an increase in earnings inequality.

The results of estimating these models are presented in the next four chapters.

Notes

1. Computed from data presented in Table No. 585 of *Statistical Abstract of the United States, 1991*.
2. See, for example, Galster, McCorkhill, and Gopalan (1988); Henle (1972); Henle and Ryscavage (1980); Ryscavage and Henle (1990); Cloutier (1997).
3. Because the census does not publish household Gini coefficients by MSA, these data (and all the other Gini coefficients used in this study) were computed by the author from the 5 percent PUMS sample.
4. The reasons for selecting MSAs as the geographic units of analysis in this study are discussed in pp. 11–13 of Chapter 1.
5. Cutler and Katz (1992) examine the effects of changes in factor shares. They find no evidence that the proportion of income distributed as earnings or payment to labor has declined relative to capital. They do find evidence of a shift in how returns on capital are paid out, however. They find that a higher proportion of returns on capital were distributed as dividends rather than retained in firms during the 1980s than in previous years.
6. The percentage change is computed as the difference between the 1990 and 1980 values divided by the 1980 value.

5   Sources of Household Income Inequality

Data from 182 metropolitan statistical areas are analyzed to measure the relationships between "within MSA" changes in the distribution of household income from 1979 to 1989 and changes in other MSA characteristics (including changes in demographic and skill composition, the characteristics of the local labor market, and the geographic structure of the metropolitan region). Data from the PUMS 5% sample from the 1980 and the 1990 U.S. censuses are used to compile shares of MSA household income accruing to each quintile and Gini coefficients for income and earnings distributions among households, workers, and various demographic subgroups in each of the 182 MSAs.

These analyses show that although MSAs that experienced increases in earnings inequality had significantly greater increases in income inequality among households, other MSA characteristics had significant associations with rising inequality. Increases in the relative amount of employment (represented by increases in the employment-to-population ratio) and changes in the distribution of workers across households frequently influence the effects of rising earnings inequality on household income inequality within MSAs.

This chapter presents the analyses of the MSA Gini coefficient of household income and of the share of MSA household income accruing to each quintile.

HOUSEHOLD INCOME DISTRIBUTION

Table 5.1 reports the correlates of changes in Gini coefficients for household income in the 182 metropolitan areas between 1979 and 1989.[1] The results of three different specifications are presented. The first, called the basic model, includes changes in demographic structure (age, race, gender, household size), skill composition (median education and the Gini coefficient on the distribution of years of education

Table 5.1 Changes in Household Income Gini Coefficients for 182 MSAs, 1979 to 1989[a]

Independent variables	Basic model	Adds earners per household	Adds local labor market and growth[b]
Demographic			
Change in % female-headed hh.	0.181	0.110	0.106
	(4.54)	(2.77)	(3.24)
	0.320	*0.193*	*0.187*
Change in % no-earner hh.		0.106	0.051
		(3.12)	(1.66)
		0.322	*0.153*
Change in % multiple-earner hh.		−0.066	0.108
		(0.87)	(1.47)
		−0.074	*0.121*
Change in % pop.	−0.011	−0.007	−0.003
African American	(−1.40)	(−0.75)	(−0.53)
	−0.83	*−0.042*	*−0.026*
Change in % elderly-headed hh.	0.041	−0.017	−0.017
	(1.50)	(−0.62)	(−0.73)
	0.099	*−0.041*	*−0.040*
Change in mean persons per hh.	−0.239	−0.270	−0.248
	(−7.29)	(−8.75)	(−9.62)
	−0.466	*−0.528*	*−0.484*
Skill			
Change in median education	−0.034	0.028	−0.018
	(−0.52)	(0.44)	(−0.35)
	−0.027	*0.022*	*−0.014*
Change in education Gini	0.034	0.052	0.016
	(0.89)	(1.43)	(0.52)
	0.054	*0.082*	*0.025*
Local labor market			
Change in earnings Gini			0.542
			(7.84)
			−0.283
Change in employment-to-			−0.336
population ratio			(−4.36)
			−0.283

Table 5.1 (continued)

Independent variables	Basic model	Adds earners per household	Adds local labor market and growth[b]
Other			
Change in ratio of % work/% live in central city	0.011 (0.72) *0.037*	0.005 (0.30) *0.015*	0.002 (0.13) *0.005*
Population in 1980 (in 10,000s)	0.108 (4.59) *0.254*	0.126 (5.73) *0.298*	0.059 (2.86) *0.134*
Change in residential segregation index[c]	0.001 (1.48) *0.078*	0.000 (0.95) *0.047*	0.000 (0.50) *0.023*
1980 Household income Gini	−0.707 (−5.54) *−0.373*	−0.497 (−3.78) *−0.262*	−0.653 (−6.01) *−0.345*
Change in residents in central city	−0.016 (−0.48) *−0.025*	−0.012 (−0.40) *−0.019*	0.038 (−0.40) *−0.058*
South Central U.S.A.	0.026 (3.37) *0.209*	0.014 (1.79) *0.109*	0.004 (0.58) *0.025*
Constant	0.287 (5.20)	0.210 (3.62)	0.290 (5.79)
Adj. R^2	0.57	0.63	0.76

[a] The top number in each set of three is the regression coefficient. Significance is defined as a t–statistic absolute value of less than 1.64. Numbers in parentheses are t–statistics; numbers in italics are beta (standardized) coefficients.

[b] This specification includes several independent variables highly correlated with economic growth that had coefficients close to zero and were also highly insignificant. These were the change in the percentage of MSA population migrated into the MSA in the last five years, percentage change in mean per capita income, percentage change in MSA population, and MSA boundary changed.

[c] Four New England MSAs did not have a segregation index. For these MSAs, the sample median index was used for the residential segregation index and a dummy variable was included. The coefficients at the dummy variable were small and highly insignificant.

among persons 25–64 years of age), and structural characteristics (whether located in the South Central region, the 1980 household income Gini coefficient for the MSA, and changes in the proportions of residents living in the central city, in the proportions of metropolitan jobs to residents in the central city, and in the levels of residential segregation).

The second specification, "adds earners per household," includes another demographic factor: changes in the household formation decisions of earners or in the labor supply decisions of household members (changes in the proportions of households that include no earners and that include more than one earner). The number of earners per household is the result of a combination of family and work decisions by individuals and of the availability of jobs. The number of earners in a household, then, is determined by the labor force participation decisions of household members, by the household formation decisions of members of the labor force, and by the availability of jobs (that is, the strength of the local labor market).

The third specification adds to the column-2 specification the effects of the local labor market by adding changes in the Gini coefficients for wages across all wage and salary earners in each MSA and changes in the ratio of total metropolitan employment to population aged 25–64. The changes in the earnings Ginis fully measure the association between household income inequality and any changes in the distributions of earnings alternatives in the metropolitan area, while changes in the employment-to-population ratios reflect changes in the overall tightness of the labor market.[2] This specification also includes a demographic characteristic (change in the growth in the proportion of in-migrants) and several structural characteristics (growth in population, growth in mean income, and whether the boundary of the MSA changed between 1980 and 1990) that are highly correlated with one another and with economic growth.

By comparing the coefficients of these specifications, one can infer the robustness of the results and the sensitivity of the correlation between changes in an independent variable and in the inequality of household income to the other characteristics included in the estimation. The additional variables permit assessment of the pathways through which changes in metropolitan characteristics affect inequality. The coefficients in the first column show the relationships between household income inequality and demographic and skill compositions and geographic structure of the MSA without controlling either for growth or local labor market conditions. The second column's coefficients show these same relationships adding the combined effects of changes in employment opportunities, labor supply decisions of household members, and household formation decisions by wage earners (which are all reflected in the number of earners per household). The third column's coefficients, by adding controls for local labor market conditions and economic growth, allow us to interpret the coefficients of earners per household as the effect of either household formation decisions by earners or labor supply decisions by household members.

Demographic Structure

The demographic structure of an MSA is significantly correlated with the extent of inequality in the MSA. MSAs with growth in the proportion of households headed by women had significant increases in household income inequality. An MSA whose proportion of households headed by women was one standard error above the mean MSA proportion had growth in household income inequality that was 0.32 standard error of the mean MSA inequality when there were no controls for local labor market conditions, economic growth, or household labor force participation and 0.187 standard error above the mean when all of those factors were controlled. A comparison of the correlations between the MSA proportions of female-headed households and MSA household income inequality varies with the controls for local labor market conditions, economic growth, and household labor force participation. The decrease in the size of the effect between the first two columns arises from the addition of controls for the number of earners per household. Obviously, female-headed households have fewer earners than couple-headed households, or even male-headed households. Almost half of the correlation between changes in the MSA proportion of households that are female-headed and MSA household income inequality arises because female-headed households have fewer earners; the remainder arises from the lower incomes of women.

There is also a substantial interaction between the proportion of female-headed households, the number of earners per household, and the overall employment-to-population ratio (which reflects the tight-ness of the local labor market).[3] The effect of the proportion of house-holds with female heads declines slightly when the employ-ment-to-population ratio is included (compare the beta coefficient in Table 5.1, second and third columns). Because only about half of the correlation between income inequality and number of earners per household arises from differential tightness of the local labor market (third column vs. second), the MSA household formation patterns of earners or the MSA labor force participation decisions of household members are associated with MSA household income distribution.

Increases in the MSA proportion of no-earner households are sig-nificantly correlated with increased MSA inequality. The effect of multiple-earner households is not significant and varies in sign between the second and third columns. When we control for labor market tightness with the employment-to-population variable (third column), then the coefficient for multiple-earner households shows the income distributional effects of household formation decisions of earn-ers. These decisions within an MSA have a statistically insignificant but positive correlation with MSA household income inequality. When we do not control for labor market tightness (second column), the coef-ficient for multiple-earner households is negative, indicating that increasing proportions of such households are correlated with decreas-ing MSA inequality; but that effect arises from multiple-earner house-holds being more prevalent in MSAs with tighter labor markets (note the 0.74 correlation coefficient reported in footnote 3).

An MSA with a mean number of persons per household one stan-dard error above other MSAs had household income inequality 0.466 standard error lower than other MSAs under the basic model and by as much as 0.528 standard error when controls for numbers of earners per household are added. This result is sensitive to the variables measuring inequality and to those included in the analyses. A related analysis presented later in this chapter (p. 111) does not show such strong corre-lation between household size and inequality.

The effects of in-migration or of population growth on inequality were negligible; these variables were included in the regression analy-ses but are not reported in Table 5.1, column 3. The coefficient of the change in the proportion of in-migrants was small, positive, and statistically insignificant, and the coefficient of change in population was small, negative, and statistically insignificant.

While MSAs experiencing an increase in the proportion of African Americans in the population or in households headed by persons over age 65 in their populations tended toward more income equality, these effects were also small and not statistically significant.

Skill Composition

The influence of the supply of skills in the local market is captured by the median years of educational attainment of the population aged 25 to 64 and by the equality of the distribution as reflected in the Gini coefficient computed on the highest year of educational attainment for those residents of the MSA. Neither MSA median education nor the education Gini is significantly correlated with MSA household income inequality.

Katz and Revenga (1989) have argued that wage/salary differences associated with education are less likely to occur in tighter labor markets. In support of their argument, the effect of the educational Gini coefficient on the household income Gini coefficient increases when the controls for number of workers per household (a measure of labor market tightness) are added (second column).[4]

Structural Characteristics

The economic and structural characteristics of the MSA are significantly associated with MSA household income distribution, and these results are consistent with previous studies. Several alternative specifications are analyzed, some including and some excluding variables that reflect growth rates in the MSAs. A comparison of the coefficients and of the adjusted R^2 across those analyses indicate that metropolitan growth does not have any statistically significant effect on MSA changes in household income inequality once MSA labor market characteristics are controlled. Household incomes in South Central[5] MSAs do not have a different rate of change in inequality between 1979 and 1989 after controls for number of earners (second column) and local labor market conditions (third column) are added.

MSA population in 1980 is strongly associated with rising household income inequality: larger MSAs experienced more growth in income inequality. Because the effect in the third column (coefficient of 0.059, beta coefficient of 0.134) is about half that in the first and second columns, however, the effect is partially due to differences in earnings inequality and labor market tightness in larger metropolitan areas. Larger MSAs have greater growth in earnings inequality and in overall labor market tightness, and both of these MSA characteristics are associated with increases in household income inequality. The next chapter examines the relationship between earnings inequality and a variety of MSA characteristics, including population size.

Neither changes in the proportion of the MSA population residing in the central city, in the ratio of the central city's share of MSA employment to the central city share of MSA residents, nor in the residential segregation index by race have significant effects on changes in MSA income inequality. There is no evidence here that residential segregation by race or spatial distributions of jobs and residents are contributing to increases in MSA income inequality.

There are noticeable, albeit insignificant, effects of local labor market conditions on skill and structural characteristics (determined by comparing the coefficients in columns two and three). The positive effects of median education level, inequality of the educational distribution, southern location, and the ratio of the percentage of MSA jobs in the city to residents in the city decline when labor market effects are included.

Labor Market Characteristics

Not surprisingly, the equality of the MSA distribution of earnings across individual workers is strongly associated with the equality of the MSA distribution of total income across households. A one-standard-error increase in the earnings Gini for all MSA workers between 1979 and 1989 is associated with a 0.365 standard error increase in the MSA household income Gini. Increases in the MSA employment-to-population ratio, representing increasing tightness of the labor market, are associated with significant decreases in MSA household income inequality. A one-standard-error increase in the employment-to-population ratio decreases the MSA household income Gini by 0.283 standard error.

The more interesting result is the finding that changes in household formation patterns are so correlated with the changes in the distribution of household income. While changes in local labor market conditions (the distribution of earnings among individuals and the employment-to-population ratio) have substantial and arguably greater effects, the demographic structure is almost as important (if not more so) and is associated with a substantial proportion of the variation across metropolitan areas in changes in household income inequality. The most important correlates of intermetropolitan variation (as indicated by the size of the standardized coefficient in the third column of Table 5.1), are changes in the number of persons in a household, the Gini coefficient for earnings distributions, the 1980 Gini coefficient for household income (reflecting regression toward the mean), changes in the employment-to-population ratio, the proportion of households headed by women, and the proportion of households with no earners.

There are two reasons why this analysis, using the MSA as the market economy, finds household formation to be important when Blank and Card (1993) and Cutler and Katz (1992), using the nation as the economy, did not. First, this analysis includes a more varied set of measures of household formation, including the number of persons per household and the number of earners per household; and second, as there is greater variability in the included household characteristics among MSAs (see Table 3.3) than across years in the nation, this study provides a more sensitive and powerful test of the effects of macro household formation patterns on inequality.

Connections between Wage Inequality and Household Income Inequality in Selected MSAs

Table 5.2 returns us to the selected MSAs introduced in Chapter 3 and allows us to continue the comparisons of their actual and predicted household income Gini coefficients, their earnings Gini coefficients, their employment-to-population ratios, and their household characteristics in light of the patterns revealed in the more systematic statistical analysis. The predicted changes in household income inequality are closer to the actual change than was the change in the earnings inequality for all MSAs other than Norfolk. (For Chicago, Los Angeles, and Philadelphia, the changes in earnings inequality are comparable to the predicted changes in household income.)

The first group includes metropolitan areas where changes in earnings inequality are close to changes in household income inequality. Chicago had the greatest difference in this group between changes in household income inequality and earnings inequality. Relative to Los Angeles and Dallas that follow, Chicago had greater growth in employment but concentrated that growth in multi-earner households. Los Angeles had less growth in employment but more evenly distributed it among households, possibly accounting for the closer connection between earnings and household income inequalities. Dallas had a relatively large growth in no-earner households, but the increase in household size and the relatively smaller increase in households headed by unmarried women accounted for earnings inequality more closely tracking household income inequality. San Diego and Norfolk had substantial growth in relative employment that appears to arise from increased numbers of earners within multi-earner households. This can happen if teenagers in lower-income households take jobs and young adult children stay with their employed parents so as to decrease single-earner, low-income households. The relative increase in household size in San Diego and the modest decrease in Norfolk are consistent with this pattern. The predicted inequality was closer to the actual when labor mar-

Table 5.2 Changes in MSA Income Inequality and Household Characteristics 1979–1989 (%)

MSA	Household income Gini			Change in					
	Actual change	Change predicted by basic model	Change predicted by adding labor market	Earnings Gini	Employment/ population ratio	Proportion no-earner hh.	Proportion multi-earner hh.	Proportion female-headed hh.	Mean persons per hh.
Group A									
Chicago	8.8	13.1	11.7	5.9	5.8	4.2	6.0	15.2	-2.9
Los Angeles	7.0	7.9	8.8	6.5	2.5	4.5	-0.4	8.1	10.4
Dallas	5.9	5.4	4.8	5.5	2.8	11.3	-0.1	4.6	20.3
San Diego	2.4	4.7	2.2	7.0	8.8	8.9	-9.2	13.0	4.0
Norfolk	-1.1	8.2	3.5	-0.9	10.3	7.8	-11.0	14.2	-5.1
Group B									
Pittsburgh	23.7	17.0	19.7	10.1	9.4	20.3	6.2	19.7	-25.1
Buffalo	16.9	14.5	15.0	4.2	9.7	15.8	10.6	10.2	-24.2
Newark	16.3	12.5	12.4	4.0	7.4	9.3	-12.1	12.1	-20.9
Johnstown	14.5	13.6	10.7	0.6	17.3	11.6	12.5	11.0	-25.0
New York	9.1	8.7	8.6	6.1	3.7	11.3	-16.0	15.9	2.8
Philadelphia	4.2	9.2	6.3	2.8	12.4	-13.5	15.7	4.8	-3.3
Group C									
Lowell	27.9	28.0	22.4	-2.3	1.4	48.7	2.5	76.2	-12.7
Lafayette	18.6	15.7	15.6	2.6	-1.7	45.9	-11.8	26.4	-24.7
Raleigh	1	14.1	11.1	-0.9	5.6	1.6	3.4	12.1	-22.7
Lawrence	6.3	2.7	6.6	-0.7	-3.5	16.8	-0.2	20.7	4.4
Lincoln	3.3	4.1	4.1	-0.4	0.6	18.2	2.8	6.3	0.5

kets were included, indicating the relatively greater importance of labor markets in these two areas.

In group B (the Mid-Atlantic MSAs), the increases in household income inequality in New York City and in Philadelphia were closer to their increases in earnings inequality than was the case for other MSAs in the region. New York City experienced a slight increase in average household size, while Newark and Buffalo experienced substantial decreases; this factor is the most obvious reason for the contrast between these MSAs. Philadelphia had little increase in disparities in either wages and salaries or in household income, in contrast to Pittsburgh (which had large increases in both) and to Johnstown (which had no increase in wage and salary disparity but a substantial increase in household income disparity). Philadelphia had a substantial decrease in the proportion of households with no earners, little growth in female-headed households, and very little decrease in average household size. In contrast, Johnstown, Pittsburgh, Newark, and Buffalo experienced substantial drops in average household size.

Group C shows the small MSAs that experienced slight decreases in earnings inequality but increases in household income inequality. First, compare the two former Massachusetts mill towns, Lawrence and Lowell, in light of the general patterns. In Lawrence, the increasing equality of wages was accompanied by a drop of 3.5 percent in the proportion of persons 25 to 64 years of age who are employed. That decrease in employment was not evenly distributed across households; there was a substantial increase, 16.8 percent, in no-earner households and only a slight decrease, 0.2 percent, in multi-earner households. Lowell had a slightly greater decrease in earnings inequality, but a substantially larger increase in household income inequality. Although there was slight growth in the proportion employed (1.4 percent), employment changes, as in Lawrence, resulted in a 48.7 percent increase in the proportion of no-earner households (from 6.7 percent to 9.9 percent of all households). There was also a dramatic 76.2 percent increase in the proportion of female-headed households (moving from 18 percent to 32 percent of all households). Lowell and Lawrence also differ in the changes in household size, with Lowell decreasing its household size 12.7 percent, from an average of 3.3 persons to 2.9 persons, while Lawrence increased its average 4.4 percent, from 2.6 to 2.8 persons. Both Lowell and Lawrence have rising disparities in their household income distribution relative to the changes in wage and salary disparities; the increases in household income inequality were correlated, however, with their shifting household structures. The greater difference between wage and salary and household income disparities occurred in Lowell. This difference can be attributed to Lowell's greater growth in female-headed and no-earner households and the drop in average household size.

Lincoln, Nebraska, and Raleigh, North Carolina, are two mid-size state capitals that also experienced minor decreases in earnings disparity but growth in household income disparity. Unlike the two Massachusetts MSAs, both of these MSAs have increasing proportions of their adult population employed. Lincoln's growth in no-earner households "accounted" for its growing household income disparity in the presence of decreasing earnings disparity and increasing employment. While Raleigh's employment growth was more evenly shared across households, Raleigh experienced a decline in average household size.

Finally, Lafayette, Louisiana, is an MSA that experienced a slight increase in earnings inequality and a substantial increase in household income inequality. The divergence in the two measures is almost as large as for Lowell. Lafayette had a slight decrease in employment, a sizeable increase in the proportion of no-earner households, and (like Lowell) a decrease in average household size.

These examples illustrate the effects of MSA demographic structure in mediating the influence of the local labor market on household income inequality.

Distribution of Household Income by Quintile

Income inequality (as measured by the Gini coefficient) may change because of shifts occurring within the distribution of income among the upper segments of the distribution as well as from changes that move income from the upper segments to the bottom segments.

Examples of MSA Income Shares Accruing to Quintiles

Figure 5.1 illustrates the share of 1989 MSA household income that accrued to the selected MSAs. The chart shows that the greater household inequality for Los Angeles, New York City, and Lafayette (Figure 3.1a) largely arises from the higher income shares accruing to the top or fifth quintile. Lowell, Lincoln, and Raleigh, which have more equal distributions of household income (Figure 3.1b), have particularly low shares accruing to the top quintile. At least for these selected MSAs, it appears that the top quintile share contributes heavily to the level of overall income inequality.

Table 5.3 reports the 1979 to 1989 percentage change in those shares for the selected MSAs. Figure 5.1 shows that almost half of MSA household income accrues to the households in the top fifth of the income distribution, and Table 5.3 shows that their share increases in each of the selected MSAs in the 1980s, except for Norfolk and Lincoln. Norfolk experienced a decrease in overall inequality, and Lincoln had the lowest rate of increase of these MSAs (see Figure 3.2). The shares of the fourth quintiles decreased for every MSA except the Massachusetts former mill towns, Lawrence and Lowell. The shares of the third quintiles decreased for every MSA except for Lincoln and Norfolk, which had two of the lowest three values for household income Gini change.

Figure 5.1 Household Income Quintile Shares for Selected MSAs

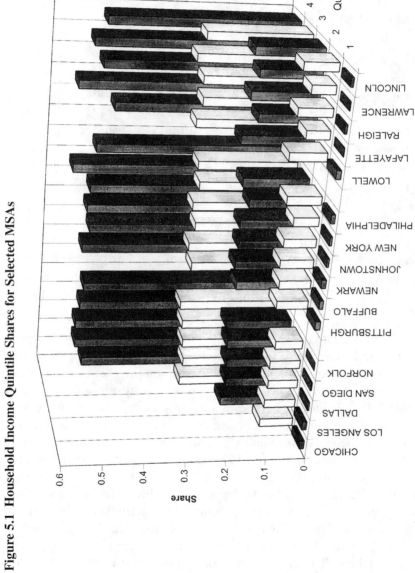

Table 5.3 Absolute Changes in Quintile Shares, 1979–1989

MSA	Quintile 1	2	3	4	5
Group A					
Chicago	–0.0018	–0.0052	–0.0132	–0.0153	0.0355
Los Angeles	–0.0040	–0.0071	–0.0096	–0.0123	0.0330
Dallas	–0.0068	–0.0152	–0.0142	–0.0103	0.0464
San Diego	0.0027	0.0070	–0.0001	–0.0112	0.0015
Norfolk	0.0000	0.0074	0.0039	–0.0079	–0.0035
Group B					
Pittsburgh	–0.0043	–0.0137	–0.0227	–0.0167	0.0573
Buffalo	–0.0047	–0.0088	–0.0132	–0.0085	0.0353
Newark	–0.0049	–0.0085	–0.0132	–0.0155	0.0421
Johnstown	–0.0065	–0.0079	–0.0108	–0.0068	0.0319
New York	–0.0066	–0.0120	–0.0099	–0.0109	0.0394
Philadelphia	0.0018	0.0056	–0.0028	–0.0130	0.0084
Group C					
Lowell	–0.0035	–0.0414	–0.0160	0.0093	0.0616
Lafayette	–0.0078	–0.0249	–0.0215	–0.0019	0.0561
Raleigh	0.0044	0.0081	–0.0012	–0.0133	0.0020
Lawrence	–0.0117	–0.0208	–0.0150	0.0057	0.0418
Lincoln	0.0062	0.0111	0.0006	–0.0113	–0.0066

To investigate the segments of the income distribution that account for the tendencies of the distribution to converge or diverge, changes in metropolitan characteristics were regressed on the change in the share of each quintile in the income distribution. The results are reported in Table 5.4. (Chapter 7 examines intermetropolitan variation in the poverty rate, another way of examining the effects of inequality on the bottom of the income distribution.) The dependent variable in this analysis is the 1989 share minus the 1979 share accruing to the quintile; it reflects the absolute change in percent share, not the percentage change in share. Table 5.1 analyzed the percentage change in the income Gini coefficient.[6] Also, in Table 5.4, I control for the 1980 quintile share for each quintile. This is comparable to the approach in Table 5.1 where I control for the 1980 Gini coefficient, but these are different independent variables. The differences in the dependent variable specification

Table 5.4 Changes in Share Accruing to Income Quintiles for 182 Metropolitan Areas, 1979–1989[a,b]

Independent variables	Quintile 1 (lowest)	2	3	4	5 (highest)
Demographic					
Change in % female-headed hh.	−0.13 (−2.78) −0.250	−0.034 (−2.51) −0.224	−0.013 (−2.05) −0.145	0.013 (2.14) 0.222	0.045 (2.30) 0.182
Change in % no-earner hh.	−0.003 (0.70) 0.094	−0.018 (−1.50) −0.206	−0.022 (−3.80) −0.445	0.006 (1.06) 0.163	0.036 (2.00) 0.251
Change in multiple-earner hh.	−0.008 (−0.77) −0.099	−0.066 (−2.17) −0.279	−0.036 (−2.56) −0.264	0.032 (2.23) 0.331	0.082 (1.83) 0.210
Change in % pop. African American	-0.000 (-0.00) -0.000	−0.001 (−0.20) −0.016	−0.002 (−1.94) −0.119	0.000 (0.22) 0.020	0.003 (0.75) 0.051
Change in % elderly-headed hh.	−0.001 (−0.27) −0.023	0.013 (1.40) −0.123	0.009 (1.93) 0.134	−0.006 (−1.22) −0.124	−0.016 (−1.16) −0.090
Change in mean persons per hh.	−0.004 (−1.11) −0.081	0.007 (0.66) 0.048	0.002 (0.38) 0.022	−0.001 (−0.28) −0.023	−0.003 (−0.17) −0.011
Skill					
Change in median education	0.008 (1.17) 0.075	−0.005 (−0.22) −0.14	−0.011 (−1.09) −0.055	−0.017 (−1.67) −0.123	0.025 (−1.23) −0.078
Change in education Gini	0.011 (0.15) 0.011	0.011 (0.95) 0.067	0.008 (1.42) 0.081	0.005 (1.01) 0.081	−0.022 (−1.23) −0.078
Local labor market					
Change in earnings Gini	−0.018 (−1.78) −0.136	−0.083 (−2.87) −0.212	−0.093 (−7.02) −0.410	−0.045 (−3.23) −0.281	0.244 (5.76) 0.376
Change in employment-to-population ratio	0.034 (3.22) 0.327	0.107 (3.36) 0.339	0.045 (3.08) 0.249	−0.032 (−2.17) −0.253	−0.153 (−3.28) −0.295
Other					
Change in ratio of % work/ % live in central city	−0.002 (−0.98) −0.061	−0.000 (−0.00) −0.000	−0.000 (−0.05) −0.002	−0.001 (−0.62) −0.044	0.004 (0.50) 0.028

(continued)

Table 5.4 (continued)

Independent variables	Quintile 1 (lowest)	2	3	4	5 (highest)
Population 1980	−0.000	0.000	−0.000	−0.001	0.001
	(−0.05)	(0.22)	(−1.24)	(−1.97)	(1.03)
	−0.004	0.017	−0.073	−0.169	0.068
Change in residential	−0.001	0.0003	0.0002	−0.0001	−0.0006
segregation index	(1.16)	(1.96)	(2.57)	(−0.72)	(−2.25)
	0.087	0.145	0.151	−0.061	−0.148
Change in residents in	−0.011	0.035	0.012	−0.008	−0.049
central city	(2.99)	(3.26)	(2.35)	(−1.60)	(−3.04)
	0.189	0.208	0.119	−0.118	−0.156
South Central U.S.A.	−0.002	−0.005	−0.002	0.001	0.008
	(−2.52)	(−2.07)	(−1.28)	(0.72)	(2.00)
	−0.200	−0.163	−0.080	0.065	0.141
Share of quintile in 1980	−0.159	−0.200	−0.136	−0.146	−0.134
	(−3.09)	(−3.84)	(−2.97)	(−2.08)	(2.00)
	−0.246	−0.274	−0.195	−0.157	−0.198
Constant	0.003	0.019	0.020	0.031	0.068
	(1.44)	(2.44	(2.70)	(1.66)	(2.49)
Adj. R^2	0.35	0.41	0.63	0.30	0.53

[a] Controlling for growth and local labor market.
[b] Numbers in parentheses are t-statistics; numbers in italics are beta (or standardized) coefficients.

and in the 1980 level dependent variable result in a different specification that can affect the results.

Table 5.4 reports the effects of metropolitan characteristics on changes in quintile shares of MSA residents using the specification that includes growth and local labor market conditions, similar to the final column in Table 5.1. While there is substantial agreement between the results reported in Tables 5.1 and Table 5.4 on the important correlates of changes in household income inequality within MSAs, there are also some important differences which arise from the slightly different specifications. The sensitivity of results to these specifications, both of which seem reasonable, suggest caution in interpreting the results for those areas where there is disagreement.

Demographic Structure

Most of the demographic variables affect the shares accruing to the quintiles comparably to their effect on overall household income inequality, as measured by the Gini coefficient. Consistent with the analysis in Table 5.1, Table 5.4 shows that increases in the MSA proportion of female-headed households are correlated with decreases in the proportion of MSA income accruing to the bottom three quintiles and increases in the top two quintiles. Similarly, Table 5.4 shows that increasing proportions of no-earner households or of multi-earner households had similar effects; increases in either of these MSA proportions correlate with decreases in the share accruing to the middle quintiles (second and third) and an increase in the share accruing to the top two quintiles. Changes in this proportion are not significantly correlated with changes in the bottom quintile's share. These results are also consistent with increases in these household categories increasing overall MSA household income inequality.

Although increases in household size within an MSA increased the shares of the second and third quintiles and decreased the shares going to the outlying quintiles, the variable has no statistically significant correlation in the quintile share analyses. This is quite surprising given the strong significance of this variable in Table 5.1. The sensitivity of household size to the specification of the analysis warrants caution. In Chapter 7, a significant negative correlation between household size and the MSA poverty rate is demonstrated. Because households in poverty are only a portion (roughly half, on average) of the households in the bottom quintile, the effects of household size on the Gini coefficient may not be obvious from data as aggregated as quintile data. The different results with respect to household size in Tables 5.1 and 5.4, however, indicate that we cannot conclude that MSAs with decreases in household size experienced rising inequality.

Skill Composition

As in the case of the household income Gini, the shares of MSA income accruing to each of the five quintiles are not significantly associated with MSA changes in either the median level of education or its distribution across the adult population. MSAs with increases in educational inequality had less growth in the share of income accruing to their top quintile and more growth in the shares of the other quintiles, although these results are statistically insignificant.

Structural Characteristics

Large MSAs, measured by population in 1980, had greater decreases in the shares of their bottom four quintiles and increases in the share of their top quintiles. The positive association found in Table 5.1 between MSA population size and changes in the household income Gini arises primarily from the correlation between population size and the income share of the top quintile. Also, for both the analysis of quintile shares and the household income Gini, the effect of population size arises in part from the differences in the local labor market changes in larger MSAs. Population size has less effect on quintile shares after controlling for local labor market conditions and for growth than when these variables are not included.[7]

The distribution of population and jobs between city and suburbs is also of significance. More centralized urban areas had greater growth in the income shares of the lower three-fifths of the household income distribution. MSAs experiencing relative increases in the proportion of residents residing in the central city had greater growth in the income share of their bottom three quintiles and less growth in their top two quintiles, with the greatest changes in the first, second, and fifth quintiles. Increases in the ratio of the share of jobs in the central city to the share of residents in the central city should favor the lower quintiles if poorer households are more likely to reside in the central city and if proximity to jobs increases income. There was no evidence of such an effect here.[8]

Increases in racial segregation of residential areas reduces the share accruing to the top quintile and increases the share accruing to the second and third quintiles. These results are surprising in light of Table 5.1, where this variable had no effect on overall household income inequality. As with household size, the different results from the two specifications require caution in interpretation.

MSAs with more inequality in 1980 experienced less growth in inequality in the 1980s. When the share of the quintile in 1980 was higher, the quintile share declined between 1980 and 1990, showing a tendency to regress to the mean over time.

Labor Market Characteristics

MSAs with increasing earnings inequality had greater shares of income accruing to households in the top quintile at the expense of all other quintiles. One standard error of increase in the MSA earnings Gini was associated with a 0.376 standard-error increase in the income share accruing to the top quintile of households and a reduction of 0.410 standard error in the share accruing to the middle (third) quintile.

For MSAs with tightening labor markets (employment-to-population ratio increases), the income shares accruing to the bottom three quintiles of households increased at the expense of the shares accruing to the top two quintiles. The share accruing to the bottom quintile increased more in MSAs with tightening labor markets than in those with decreasing earnings inequality.[9] The opposite is the case for the top quintile.

SUMMARY

Several factors account for intermetropolitan variations in the equality of the household income distribution. The principal findings are as follows:

- Household income inequality within MSAs increased during the 1980s.

- MSAs experiencing changes in the local labor market also experienced changes in income inequality.

  - MSAs with rising earnings inequality experienced rising household income inequality. In MSAs with increases in earnings inequality, the share of the top quintile increased and the shares of all others decreased, particularly the second and third quintiles. But, MSA increases in household income inequality exceeded MSA increases in earnings inequality.

- In most MSAs, employment-to-population ratios increased. For MSAs where this ratio increased at a higher rate, household income inequality decreased relative to other MSAs. MSAs with greater increases in the employment-to-population ratio had relatively greater increases in the shares of the bottom three quintiles and relatively greater decreases in the shares of the top two quintiles.

- As the effects of increases in the employment-to-population ratio offset the effects of rising earnings inequality on household income inequality in most MSAs, overall changes in the local labor market do not account for the growth in household income inequality in U.S. metropolitan areas.

• MSAs with demographic shifts—in particular changes in the kinds of households formed—had greater changes in income inequality.

- MSAs with increases in no-earner households and in multi-earner households had decreases in the share of the second and third or middle income quintiles of households and increases in the share of the top 40 percent of households.

- MSAs with increases in the proportion of households headed by women experienced decreases in the shares of income accruing to the bottom 60 percent of the household income distribution, and increases in the share for the upper 40 percent.

• MSAs with changes in the distribution of jobs and residents between their central city and suburbs and in the extent of residential segregation by race experienced little change in household income inequality.

• MSAs with changes in educational attainment, including increases in the average level of educational attainment and changes in the distribution of educational attainment, had little change in household income inequality, regardless of whether labor market conditions are considered.

- MSAs with larger central cities (relative to the suburbs) had less increase in inequality due to greater increases in income shares for the bottom three quintiles and a decrease for the top quintile. The lower 60 percent of the household income distribution fared better in metropolitan areas with larger central cities.

Notes

1. Because larger Gini coefficients indicate a more unequal distribution, a negative coefficient for a variable indicates that the variable is associated with decreasing inequality and a positive coefficient with increasing inequality. Table 5.1 reports the regression coefficient, the t-statistic (in parentheses), and the standardized, or beta, coefficient (in italics). The beta coefficient represents the association between a one-standard-error change in the independent variable and the standard error of the dependent variable, the household income Gini for metropolitan areas. Beta coefficients are the result of a linear regression where each variable is "normalized" by subtracting its mean and dividing by its estimated standard error. The beta coefficient, then, standardizes for differences in the measurement units across the independent variables, allowing for comparisons of the relative importance of these variables.

2. Other studies (for example, Danziger [1976]), have used measures of industrial composition to reflect wage distribution and have estimated two-stage equations in order to infer the effect of the labor market on household or family income distribution. The data used here allow direct measurement of the earnings distribution available to individual workers.

3. The correlation among these four variables is:

	Female head (%)	No-earner (%)	Multi-earner (%)
No-earner	0.54		
Multi-earner	–0.45	–0.78	
Empl./pop. ratio	–0.39	–0.51	0.74

A correlation of 1.00 means that the variables are identical; of –1.00 means that one variable is the exact negative of the other; and of 0 means that they are not related in any way.

4. The third column adds the employment-to-population ratio for persons 25 to 64 years of age but also adds the earnings Gini that controls for the wage effects of the educational distribution. The coefficient of the education Gini is decreased once its wage effects are held constant.

5. "South Central" includes the East South Central and the West South Central states, but not the South Atlantic (which showed no significant difference from the

rest of the nation). The states included are Kentucky, Tennessee, Alabama, Mississippi, Arkansas, Louisiana, Oklahoma, and Texas. Other regional controls were tested but were not significant.

6. The change in the Gini coefficient on household income within MSAs is most highly correlated with the change in the share accruing to the third quintile (–0.60) and the fifth quintile (0.50). Consistent with previous analyses of the Gini coefficient, the change in the Gini coefficient across MSAs is most sensitive to changes in the middle quintile and least sensitive to changes in the first and fifth quintiles. A regression of the change in quintile shares on the Gini coefficient showed the third quintile had the largest absolute coefficient (but the sign was, of course, negative).

7. These regression results are not included here but are available from the author.

8. All the coefficients (including the beta coefficients) were very close to 0, and none had t-statistics greater than an absolute value of 1.

9. See, for example, in Table 5.4, the beta coefficient for the bottom quintile's change in share is 0.327 for employment-to-population ratio and –0.136 for the earnings Gini.

6   A More Detailed Study
of Household Income and
Individual Earnings Inequality

In the last chapter, the overall relationships were defined between changes in MSA household income inequality within metropolitan areas during the 1980s, and changes in MSA household demographic characteristics and in local labor market conditions. MSAs having greater growth in earnings inequality were shown to have more growth in income inequality among households, but this relationship is strongly mediated by changes in the availability of employment, in household structure, and in the way that wage-earners are distributed among households.

In this chapter, I examine other components of those relationships, including a) the characteristics of MSAs associated with changes in earnings inequality, and b) whether MSA characteristics have similar relationships to changes in the equality of the distribution of household income within particular demographic subgroupings of the metropolitan population.

EARNINGS DISTRIBUTION

Several studies, as discussed in Chapter 2, have examined the sources of earnings inequality, and a large number have concluded that increasing demand for skills coupled with a relative decrease in the number of experienced and highly educated workers have resulted in upward movement of wages for skilled workers. These conclusions have been reached based largely on national studies. But, as is the case for household income inequality, no study has examined the characteristics of MSAs that experienced increasing earnings inequality in the 1980s.

The distribution of wages and salaries within a labor market is the result of the interactions between the demand for labor and the supply of labor. The local demand for labor is derived from the demand for the outputs of local industry. Consumer tastes and the attractiveness of the MSA as a production site affect local demand for labor. The demographic and skill characteristics of local residents affect local labor supply (and demand). The market outcome is shaped, then, by MSA demographic and skill characteristics of the labor force and by the structure of the MSA and its industrial composition. The demographic characteristics of MSAs used in the household income inequality analyses that also affect earnings inequality within MSAs are the changes in the population proportions of African Americans and of in-migrants. African-American workers have greater earnings inequality and lower wages than other workers. MSAs with more in-migrants are faster growing, and growth may affect earnings inequality.[1]

The number of workers per household and household size measures are pertinent to the income accruing to households but do not directly affect wages paid to individuals. Similarly, whether the head is over 65 or female[2] correlates with special household income situations (such as pensions, welfare, and alimony, and the labor supply decisions of household members) that are relevant to household income but not to individual wages.

The MSA skill and structural characteristics used in the household income analyses and the employment-to-population ratio (a measure of labor market tightness) may also affect the equality of the MSA earnings distribution. Increasing skill differentials within the local labor force should increase productivity differentials and therefore lead to wage differences, so an increase in the inequality of the distribution of education (as measured by the Gini coefficient of educational attainment) is expected to increase earnings inequality. Labor markets in MSAs with relatively greater increases in average education may value skills more than those in MSAs with less increase in education. If that is the case, the match between a skill set and a job may have greater effects on productivity in MSAs with greater growth in educational attainment, resulting in a correlation between increasing average education in an MSA and increasing earnings inequality. To the extent that value of skills has grown more important in production and larger or more populous MSAs have a finer division of labor (or a better match between skill of worker and task requirements), there will be greater earnings inequality in larger MSAs. Alternatively, tighter labor markets are expected to improve opportunities for less-skilled, lower-wage workers, so increases in the employment-to-population ratio are expected to reduce earnings inequality.

There are two measures that reflect the potential effects of a spatial mismatch between workers and jobs in MSAs, the residential segregation index by race and the ratio of the proportion of the MSA jobs to the proportion of the MSA residential population in the central city. If residential segregation affects job access, then there would be more wage inequality in MSAs with more segregation because the "market" cannot function as well and greater artificial wage differentials result. Lower-income households are more likely to live in the central city, and these households are more likely to include lower-wage workers. If jobs are moving to the suburbs faster than residential population, then accessible job alternatives for low-wage city workers are decreasing. Fewer jobs for low-wage workers should lower their wages. The ratio of the city's share of jobs to its share of population would then be expected to be negatively correlated with earnings inequality.

Industrial structure, specifically changes in the proportions of the workforce employed in durable goods manufacturing and in producer services, is expected to affect earnings inequality. Because the durable goods manufacturing industry has better wages for workers with less formal education and because workers in this industry are more likely to be unionized, earnings inequality is expected to be lower in this industry. MSAs with more employment growth in this industrial sector are expected to have less growth in earnings inequality. Numerous authors have alleged that the new producer services industry creates many low-paying and many high-paying jobs, with few middle-wage jobs. If this were the case, then MSAs with more employment growth in producer services would be expected to have more growth in earnings inequality.

Earnings Inequality for All Workers

The first column of Table 6.1 reports the correlates/determinants of the rates of change in MSA Gini coefficients for wage and salary income between 1979 and 1989 for all workers, the variable used to measure the wage distribution in the analyses of household income inequality. MSAs experiencing a relatively greater increase in the propor-

Table 6.1 Changes in Earnings Gini Coefficients for 182 Metropolitan Areas, 1979–1989[a]

Independent variables	All wage and salary earners	All full-time year-round earners	Management/ professionals	Men in precision and operative	Women in clerical	Producer service workers	Sales workers
Demographic							
Change in % pop. African American	-0.012	-0.019	-0.013	-0.006	0.007	0.003	-0.005
	(-1.924)	(-2.112)	(-1.410)	(-0.566)	(0.730)	(0.329)	(-0.574)
	-0.133	-0.160	-0.106	-0.032	-0.053	0.025	-0.041
Change in % pop. in-migrant	-0.020	-0.041	-0.041	-0.058	-0.029	-0.020	0.018
	(-1.447)	(-2.005)	(-1.942)	(-2.536)	(-1.389)	(-1.135)	(0.992)
	-0.107	0.160	-0.154	-0.154	-0.109	-0.091	0.075
Skill							
Change in median education	0.048	0.072	0.083	0.080	0.002	0.002	0.066
	(0.845)	(0.852)	(0.934)	(0.840)	(0.024)	(0.525)	(0.851)
	0.056	0.062	0.068	0.046	0.002	0.039	0.060
Change in education Gini	0.025	0.033	0.136	-0.023	-0.027	-0.063	-0.045
	(0.791)	(0.714)	(2.749)	(-0.433)	(-0.574)	(-1.611)	(-1.120)
	0.059	0.057	0.223	-0.027	-0.044	-0.125	-0.082
Local labor market							
Change in employment-to-population ratio	-0.121	-0.072	-0.064	-0.092	-0.086	0.071	0.166
	(-1.933)	(-0.783)	(-0.642)	(-0.886)	(-0.882)	(0.868)	(1.989)
	-0.152	-0.066	-0.055	-0.057	-0.074	0.075	0.160

Other

Change in ratio of % jobs/% residents in central city	0.017 (1.239) *0.080*	0.028 (1.378) *0.097*	0.036 (1.719) *0.121*	0.016 (0.688) *0.037*	−0.021 (−0.979) *−0.068*	−0.004 (−0.205) *−0.015*	−0.004 (−0.196) *−0.013*
Change in population	−0.019 (−0.961) *−0.085*	−0.031 (−1.020) *−0.102*	−0.036 (−1.181) *−0.113*	0.041 (1.166) *0.093*	−0.008 (−0.259) *0.024*	−0.019 (−0.698) *−0.071*	0.012 (0.471) *0.043*
Change in mean income	−0.027 (−1.894) *−0.162*	0.030 (1.397) *0.132*	0.005 (0.216) *0.020*	−0.076 (−3.054) *−0.222*	−0.046 (−1.989) *−0.188*	−0.039 (−2.028) *−0.197*	−0.026 (−1.345) *−0.120*
Change in residential segregation index	0.000 (0.072) *0.005*	−0.000 (−0.130) *−0.011*	−0.000 (−0.263) *−0.023*	−0.000 (−0.014) *−0.001*	−0.000 (−0.248) *−0.020*	0.000 (0.291) *0.024*	0.001 (1.177) *0.095*
1980 Population (in 10,000s)	0.034 (1.682) *0.118*	0.086 (2.887) *0.220*	0.048 (1.545) *0.118*	0.094 (2.792) *0.162*	0.021 (0.663) *0.050*	0.002 (0.083) *0.006*	0.021 (0.792) *0.057*
Change in residents in central city	0.026 (0.879) *0.059*	0.012 (0.271) *0.020*	0.051 (1.120) *0.081*	0.120 (2.469) *0.137*	0.122 (2.709) *0.193*	0.111 (2.931) *0.217*	0.043 (1.095) *0.076*
South Central U.S.A.	0.012 (1.748) *0.137*	0.004 (0.368) *0.034*	0.008 (0.813) *0.070*	0.015 (1.295) *0.086*	−0.009 (−0.899) *−0.077*	0.014 (1.545) *0.137*	0.009 (0.995) *0.082*

(continued)

Table 6.1 (continued)

Independent variables	All wage and salary earners	All full-time year-round earners	Management/ professionals	Men in precision and operative	Women in clerical	Producer service workers	Sales workers
1980 Earnings Gini for group	−0.369	−0.740	−0.593	−1.324	−0.871	−0.300	−1.049
	(−2.975)	(−3.643)	(−3.484)	(−8.838)	(−5.720)	(−2.647)	(−7.541)
	−0.225	−0.336	−0.270	−0.672	−0.433	−0.209	−0.519
Industrial Composition							
Change in % of employment in durable goods manufacture	−0.034	−0.026	0.006	0.055	0.004	0.026	−0.004
	(−2.461)	(−1.288)	(−0.263)	(−2.327)	(0.188)	(−1.442)	(−0.215)
	−0.178	−0.100	−0.021	−0.143	0.014	−0.116	−0.016
Change in % in producer services	−0.021	−0.045	−0.050	−0.033	−0.074	−0.055	−0.031
	(−1.346)	(−1.926)	(−2.079)	(−1.230)	(−3.052)	(−2.721)	(−1.480)
	−0.095	−0.145	−0.156	−0.072	−0.225	−0.208	−0.106
Constant	0.216	0.270	0.246	0.542	0.390	0.190	0.609
	(3.519)	(4.056)	(3.181)	(9.492)	(5.630)	(2.894)	(7.733)
Adj. R^2	0.34	0.22	0.22	0.55	0.24	0.18	0.29

[a] Numbers in parentheses are t-statistics; numbers in italics are beta or standardized coefficients.

tion of African-American households, in mean income, in employment-to-population ratio, and in durable goods manufacturing employment experienced less increase in earnings inequality. Interestingly, MSAs with growth in producer services employment experienced an insignificant decrease in inequality. Larger MSAs and those in the South Central United States had greater increases in earnings inequality. As with changes in household income inequality, there is a tendency to "regress to the mean." MSAs with larger 1980 levels of earnings inequality have less growth in inequality during the 1980s.

The results—the significance of changes in mean income and in employment-to-population ratio—are consistent with the hypothesis that economic growth decreases earnings inequality. Industrial structure also matters, although not in the way that some expect. Durable goods manufacturing industries reduce wage inequality, but producer service industries do not increase, and may decrease, inequality. There is also evidence that the supply of and demand for skilled workers matters. The positive significance of MSA population size and the positive, albeit insignificant, coefficients on changes in average education and in the Gini on educational attainment are consistent with skill changes contributing to increasing earnings inequality.

Earnings Inequality for Full-time Year-round Workers

The coefficients of the various MSA characteristics in Table 6.1 may arise because the characteristics are the cause of the change in inequality, or the change in inequality may cause the change in the characteristics, or the correlation may arise because the characteristics are correlated with other, unmeasured characteristics of the MSA. One way to understand better why these characteristics are connected to MSA wage inequality is to examine their effects on wage inequality among subsets of workers.

First, I compare the results for the distribution of earnings across all workers (column 1) to those for full-time year-round workers (column 2, which excludes part-time and part-year workers). Differences between these results can be attributed to differences in the sources of inequality for part-time or part-year workers. Variation or inequality in earnings arise from differences in hours worked, as well as from differences in rates of pay. There is significantly less variation in total work hours among full-time year-round workers than among all workers. Among full-time year-round workers, variation in wages or inequality is more likely to be attributed to differences in pay rates.

There are interesting differences between the two groups. The rate of growth in MSA per-capita income (Table 6.1, "mean income" row) is correlated with a decrease in earnings inequality among all workers, but with an insignificant increase in inequality among full-time full-year workers. This result is consistent with increases in work hours (i.e., expansion of employment) rather than changes in wage rates being the important source of MSA growth in per-capita income. MSAs with growing producer service employment have greater decreases in earnings inequality for full-time year-round workers than do MSAs with growing durable goods manufacturing employment. If employees in durable goods manufacturing are more likely than those in other industries to be full-time year-round workers, then MSAs with increases in workers in that industry would have less growth in inequality among all workers, but with less change among full-time year-round workers. In other words, MSAs with more durable goods manufacturing jobs have less earnings inequality because these workers have more work hours, not because they have higher or more equal pay rates. Similarly, if producer service industries paid wage rates that were "more equal" than other industries but had more part-time or part-year workers, MSAs with growth in the proportion of workers in producer services would have a greater decrease in inequality among full-time year-round workers than among all wage and salary workers. The results in Table 6.1 show this to be the case.

The correlation between earnings inequality and MSA size is greater for full-time workers than for all workers. Based on the same logic applied to the results for the mean income and industrial employment variables, this result is consistent with larger MSAs having less variation in hours worked but more variation in rates of pay.

The comparisons of the earnings inequality results between all workers and full-time year-round workers provide information on the relative role of work hours and pay rates in creating earnings inequality in an MSA. It appears that larger MSAs and MSAs with less producer service employment have more variation in pay rates, while MSAs with more durable goods manufacturing employment have less variation in work hours. Furthermore, MSAs experiencing greater growth in per-capita income have increasing work hours but less variation in pay rates.

Earnings Inequality within Occupations and Industries

The right-most five columns of Table 6.1 examine MSA earnings inequality among resident workers in specific occupations and industries. The independent variables are the same as for the first two columns, reflecting characteristics of the entire MSA, not of the industry or occupation group. Table 3.1 showed that producer services workers were the only group of MSA residents to experience a convergence of wages in the 1980s, with an average decrease in inequality within MSAs of 1.7 percent. Next, women in clerical occupations had the least change in earnings inequality, an increase of 0.3 percent over the decade, while the men in skilled and semi-skilled blue-collar jobs (precision and operative occupations) and the professional and management workers of both sexes have increases of 4.0 percent and 4.1 percent, respectively. For sales workers, the average MSA experienced a 2.7 percent increase in earnings inequality.

Management and professionals are a relatively highly educated group of workers, women in clerical work are in relatively homogenous jobs, men in blue-collar jobs are relatively less educated, while producer services and sales workers are in rapidly expanding industries and occupations. We can examine the characteristics of MSAs with changes in earnings inequality among these groups in order to assess whether the changes varied for occupational and industrial subgroups, and to identify the types of labor markets, or characteristics of workers, associated with different outcomes.

MSAs with increases in the proportion of African-American residents experienced the same shifts in equality of the earnings within occupations or industries as other MSAs. This may occur simply because the Gini coefficients are measured with less precision for the smaller occupational and industry groups or because the tendency for MSAs experiencing growth in the proportion of African Americans to experience less inequality overall for the workforce (Chapter 5) may arise from the differential distribution of African-American workers across industries and occupations in these MSAs, rather than from wage distribution differences within industries and occupations.

MSAs with more in-migrants experienced less growth in earnings inequality within occupation and industry groups, suggesting that in-migration (which is strongly associated with economic vitality) increases earnings equality. If expanding economies have more in-migrants and stronger markets for low-wage workers, then there is likely to be no "direct causation" between in-migration and earnings inequality; rather, the relationship is that vibrant economies have less earnings inequality.

MSAs with rising median education levels experienced no statistically significant increase in earnings inequality for any groups in Table 6.1. As the coefficients do not meet normal standards of significance, it is difficult to conclude very much from these relationships, but there is some suggestion that in those pools that include more part-time workers—women in clerical, producer services workers, sales workers, and the all workers category—MSAs with rising education have less growth in inequality. These subcategories are likely to include more highly educated persons, especially women, who work shorter hours, resulting in lower incomes. For those categories where there is less part-time work—full-time year-round workers, management and professionals, and men in blue-collar occupations—MSAs with rising education are more likely to have rising inequality; that is, the coefficient on change in median education is of greater magnitude.

MSAs with more unequally distributed education do not have more earnings inequality for all groups in Table 6.1 with the exception of managers and professionals, the most educated group. For this group, MSAs with greater educational inequality have significantly greater earnings inequality. MSAs with more growth in education also have more growth in earnings inequality for this group. This result is consistent with MSAs having rising levels of education placing a greater valuation on education/skill in production and a greater importance on skill differences or the quality of the match between skills and jobs.

MSAs with relatively greater increases in the proportion of the MSA population resident in the central city are more likely to be smaller MSAs, to have experienced increases in female-headed households, and are less likely to have increases in in-migrants, per-capita income, average education, or population (see correlation coefficients, Table A1 in the Appendix). The regression analysis shows that these same MSAs have more-unequal earnings for men in skilled and semi-skilled blue-collar occupations, for women in clerical occupations, and for producer service workers. MSAs with changes in their relative central city size have insignificantly more earnings inequality for the other groups. The results for this MSA characteristic are probably reflecting the effect of stagnant economies on inequality rather than reflecting a direct causal relationship between central city size and inequality. More stagnant economies have more wage inequality.

MSAs with growth in per-capita income have insignificant increases in earnings inequality among professionals and managers, but have less inequality, in most cases significantly less, for all other groups. Again, these results provide additional confirmation that MSAs with more economic growth have less earnings inequality.

Earnings inequality increased most in larger MSAs during the 1980s; this is especially the case for full-time year-round workers and for men in blue-collar occupations. Generally, MSAs with tightening labor markets (represented by increases in the employment-to-population ratio) have insignificantly less inequality for all subgroups; sales workers stand out as an exception.[3]

The industrial composition of an MSA, not surprisingly, is associated with increases in inequality for some subgroups and decreases for others. MSAs with more durable goods manufacturing have significantly greater earnings equality for men in blue-collar jobs. MSAs with more producer service industry employment have greater earnings equality for managers and professionals, women in clerical jobs, and all producer services workers. The implication appears to be that MSAs with larger industrial markets for a set of "occupational" skills have a more equal wage distribution among workers with those skills. This is consistent with the hypothesis that economic expansion increases wage equality. This appears to be the case both for the entire local labor market, the MSA, and for the industry market within the MSA.

Overall, MSAs with higher rates of economic growth had less growth in inequality because they experienced increasing demand for (and wages and work hours of) lower-skilled workers, and possibly they experienced changes in skill requirements and technology. Earnings inequality among workers can arise from inequality in the rate of pay or from inequality in work hours. It is apparent from the analyses presented here that variation in MSA work hours is a major contributor to MSA earnings inequality.   While MSAs with more population, increases in per-capita income, and increases in the proportion of workers employed in durable goods manufacturing had less increase in earnings inequality, an important part of this lesser increase comes from MSA total work hours (as evidenced by the much weaker role of these MSA characteristics on inequality among full-time, year-round workers).

DISTRIBUTION OF HOUSEHOLD INCOME WITHIN SUBPOPULATIONS

We learned in the previous section that subpopulations may yield important insights into the basis for the correlations observed in analyzing MSA inequality for the entire population. Analyses of subpopulations permit insight into whether a correlation between an observed MSA characteristic and inequality reflects a direct causation or reflects correlation between the observed characteristics (or set of conditions) that are affected by inequality.

Table 6.2 examines which metropolitan characteristics are associated with the household distribution of income within particular demographic subgroups: no-earner households, multi-earner households, African Americans, households whose head is over age 65, households whose head moved to the metropolitan area within the last five years, and households headed by women. The characteristics analyzed are for the entire MSA, not just for the group being studied; these characteristics, then, are the same measures as used in Table 5.1. The results are to be interpreted as showing how changes in the overall, macro-environmental characteristics of the metropolitan area are associated with changes in income inequality within the identified subpopulation.

In general, metropolitan characteristics are less correlated with metropolitan differences in the distribution of household income within these subpopulations than they are for the total population (see Table 5.1). In part, this is due to the greater error involved in the estimates of the Gini coefficient for smaller populations. The greater explanatory power of MSA characteristics for income inequality changes among the no-earner and multi-earner households subpopula-

Table 6.2 Changes in Household Income Gini Coefficients for Subpopulations, 182 Metropolitan Areas, 1979 to 1989[a]

Independent variables	African-American hh.	In-migrant hh.	Female-headed hh.	Elderly-headed hh.	No-earner hh.	Multiple-earner hh.
Demographic						
Change in % female-headed hh.	0.023	0.111	-0.009	-0.012	0.023	0.038
	(0.26)	(1.53)	(-0.50)	(-0.48)	(0.67)	(2.02)
	0.030	0.172	-0.059	-0.055	0.070	0.197
Change in % no-earner hh.	0.030	0.071	0.019	-0.036	0.029	-0.003
	(0.38)	(1.08)	(1.11)	(-1.66)	(0.93)	(-0.18)
	0.069	0.188	0.206	-0.293	0.150	-0.027
Change in % multiple-earner hh.	-0.423	-0.087	0.022	-0.037	0.181	0.002
	(-2.21)	(-0.55)	(0.52)	(-0.70)	(2.41)	(0.05)
	-0.356	0.085	0.087	-0.111	0.348	0.007
Change in % pop. African American	0.031	-0.016	0.005	0.001	0.004	-0.005
	(1.85)	(-1.14)	(1.25)	(0.22)	(0.57)	(-1.28)
	0.179	-0.106	0.125	0.021	0.050	0.104
Change in % elderly-headed hh.	-0.014	-0.018	0.004	0.005	-0.078	-0.005
	(-0.23)	(-0.36)	(0.32)	(0.31)	(-3.28)	(-0.38)
	-0.026	-0.039	0.036	0.033	-0.324	-0.035
Change in % pop. in-migrant	0.035	-0.045	0.007	0.006	0.000	0.000
	(1.10)	(-1.72)	(1.96)	(0.64)	(0.03)	(0.00)
	0.095	-0.143	0.094	0.054	0.070	0.000

(continued)

Table 6.2 (continued)

Independent variables	African-American hh.	In-migrant hh.	Female-headed hh.	Elderly-headed hh.	No-earner hh.	Multiple-earner hh.
Change in mean persons per hh.	0.073	0.001	0.020	0.008	-0.027	0.005
	(1.14)	(0.19)	(1.47)	(0.47)	(-1.07)	(0.36)
	0.111	*0.002*	*0.148*	*0.045*	*-0.093*	*0.029*
Skill						
Change in median education	0.026	-0.008	0.018	0.009	-0.073	0.066
	(0.020)	(-0.07)	(0.64)	(0.24)	(-1.39)	(2.30)
	0.016	*-0.005*	*0.052*	*0.019*	*-0.099*	*0.154*
Change in education Gini	0.135	0.038	0.018	0.052	0.062	-0.014
	(1.74)	(0.59)	(1.04)	(2.40)	(2.01)	(-0.81)
	0.162	*0.053*	*0.100*	*0.221*	*0.168*	*-0.063*
Other						
Change in ratio of % jobs/ % residents in central city	-0.030	0.043	0.004	0.005	0.004	0.018
	(-0.95)	(1.62)	(0.64)	(0.58)	(0.29)	(2.62)
	-0.073	*0.122*	*0.052*	*0.045*	*0.020*	*0.171*
Change in population	-0.96	-0.051	-0.007	-0.029	-0.011	-0.005
	(-2.16)	(-1.37)	(-0.73)	(-2.33)	(-0.61)	(-0.56)
	-0.222	*-0.136*	*-0.078*	*-0.237*	*-0.056*	*-0.048*
1980 Population (in 10,000s)	0.024	-0.058	-0.000	-0.008	0.002	0.015
	(0.65)	(-1.35)	(-0.00)	(-0.53)	(0.11)	(1.32)
	0.042	*-0.120*	*-0.000*	*-0.48*	*0.009*	*0.101*

	(1)	(2)	(3)	(4)	(5)	(6)
Change in mean income	0.044	0.071	−0.004	0.014	0.025	0.005
	(1.19)	(2.32)	(−0.50)	(1.33)	(1.70)	(0.59)
	0.132	*0.250*	*−0.058*	*0.147*	*0.170*	*0.055*
Change in residential segregation index	−0.001	0.0002	0.000	−0.001	−0.000	0.000
	(−1.05)	(0.22)	(0.28)	(−2.49)	(−0.27)	(0.10)
	−0.097	*0.019*	*0.027*	*−0.227*	*−0.022*	*0.008*
Change in residents in central city	−0.109	−0.057	0.002	0.005	−0.029	−0.002
	(−1.61)	(−1.01)	(0.16)	(0.26)	(−1.10)	(−0.13)
	−0.128	*−0.078*	*0.013*	*0.020*	*−0.078*	*−0.008*
1980 Household income Gini	−0.247	−0.386	0.067	0.135	0.447	−0.003
	(−0.90)	(−1.70)	(1.14)	(1.78)	(4.16)	(−0.05)
	−0.100	*−0.179*	*0.129*	*0.192*	*0.408*	*−0.005*
Local labor market						
Change in earnings Gini	−0.069	−0.130	0.021	0.027	0.219	0.244
	(−0.38)	(−0.87)	(0.53)	(0.54)	(3.08)	(6.28)
	−0.035	*−0.077*	*0.050*	*0.049*	*0.254*	*0.485*
Change in employment-to-population ratio	0.261	−0.220	−0.033	−0.017	−0.144	−0.020
	(0.31)	(−1.33)	(−0.76)	(−0.31)	(−1.84)	(−0.46)
	0.166	*0.163*	*−0.099*	*−0.038*	*−0.210*	*−0.049*
Adj. R^2	0.07	0.13	0.01	0.09	0.25	0.34

[a] Numbers in parentheses are t-statistics; numbers in italics are beta or standardized coefficients.

tions arises from the greater importance of labor market characteristics for these populations that are defined, after all, relative to their labor market outcomes.

MSAs with greater earnings inequality have significantly greater income inequality among multi-earner households. For these households who have multiple earners in both periods, there is less variation possible in labor supply, so wages and salaries have larger effects on inequality.

MSAs with greater change in the employment-to-population ratio and greater increases in the proportion of elderly households have significantly less income inequality among no-earner households. These results are consistent with greater MSA equality among no-earner households when they are "no-earner" by choice. Obviously, households that choose to be "no-earner" are more likely than households with earners to have incomes from other sources. With fewer households that are no-earner because no household member can find a job (more likely to be the case when there is less employment relative to population), the lower tail of the no-earner income distribution is eliminated. Similarly, when a larger share of households are headed by senior citizens, they are more likely to be no-earner because of retirement and, then, to have other income. The finding that MSAs with more earnings inequality have more income inequality for no-earners is more difficult to explain. As with employment-to-population, the effect must arise from the selection of households into the no-earner status. Local labor markets with more earnings inequality either encourage members of households from the extremes of the income distribution to withdraw from the labor force or, alternatively, encourage those in the middle to enter employment.

It is interesting that MSAs with greater growth in overall earnings inequality did not have statistically significant changes in the inequality of income among African-American, over-age-65, in-migrant, or female-headed households. MSAs with changes in the employment-to-population measure (and the correlated proportion of households who are multi-earner) also had no different income inequality for the over-65, the in-migrant and the female-headed households. These results suggest that the labor market has less effect on inequality among these groups.

MSAs with changes in the proportion of African-American households or of in-migrant households had no significant changes in the household income distribution among any of the other subpopulations. African-American household income grew more unequal in MSAs with greater growth in the African-American population; however, the distribution of household income among in-migrants grew more equal as the proportion of in-migrants in the MSA grew. Both of these effects are of borderline statistical significance.

While MSAs with increases in the proportion of households headed by women had increased inequality among no-earner households and multi-earner households (which is consistent with the overall results reported in Table 5.1), there was no effect for the other MSA subpopulations.

Households headed by persons over age 65 are very likely to have no earners. For this reason, the growth of elderly households, whose incomes are tied to pensions and other retirement income, is correlated with increased income equality among no-earner households. Similarly, the growth in no-earner households is correlated with increased income equality among over-age-65 households.

In total, the results of Table 6.2 indicate that, to the extent MSAs experiencing changes in the representation of these demographic groups have changes in overall income inequality, the association arises from the position of the group in the overall distribution, rather than from changes in the distribution of income within the group.

SUMMARY

The principal findings are that, with respect to MSA earnings inequality,

- MSAs with more variation in work hours have substantially more variation in earnings inequality.
- MSAs with more growth in earnings inequality had less economic growth. MSAs with economic growth had less variation in both pay rates and total work hours.

- MSAs with more population and those that experienced an increase, or less of a decrease, in employment in durable goods manufacturing industries experienced a decrease in earnings inequality which was mostly due to the effects on total work hours.

- Contrary to much speculation, MSAs with more growth in producer service employment reduced earnings inequality among full-time workers, and did so to a greater extent than MSAs with comparable increases in durable goods manufacturing employment.   MSAs with more producer service workers did have greater variation, or inequality, in total work hours, however.

With respect to inequality within subgroups of metropolitan populations,

- MSAs with more change in their local labor market did not have more changes in the distribution of income within African-American, over-age-65, in-migrant, or female-headed households.

Notes

1. It is also the case that the race and the migration status of a household head also apply in most cases to all other household members, so that these characteristics of household heads are also reliable as population characteristics.
2. Gender is a factor in the labor market because women earn less than men, but the extent to which women head households has no direct effects on the distribution of wages.
3. A possible reason why sales work is different is that potentially low-wage sales workers may move to other industries and occupations when the economy heats up, leaving relatively more workers whose earnings are in the middle range, thus reducing inequality.

7 Sources of MSA Poverty

As described in Chapter 4, poverty rates are another common index of how income is distributed among households. Unlike the Gini coefficient, and unlike the measures of shares of income accruing to quintiles that measure the relative position of the bottom, the middle, and the top of the distribution, the poverty index is based on the income needed by the household to purchase basic levels of food, shelter, and services. The proportion of households with incomes below the poverty level, then, reflects the proportion of households who are unable to acquire a minimal living standard; the proportion does not reflect the difference between high- and low-income households.

Based on an analysis of changes in poverty rates in metropolitan areas during the 1980s, this chapter presents evidence that MSAs with more economic growth had less growth in poverty, and MSAs with increases in earnings inequality had more growth in poverty; but MSAs of varying racial compositions, MSAs with proportionately larger central cities, and MSAs with more movement of jobs from the city to the suburbs had no differential growth in poverty.

COMPARING HOUSEHOLD INEQUALITY AND POVERTY MEASURES

While changes in the poverty rate in a metropolitan area may reflect changes in the equality of the household income distribution within the area, poverty rates and income inequality are not the same. The Gini coefficient measures changes in household income across the entire distribution of household income; the poverty rate measures the proportion of households who receive an income below a level defined as necessary to maintain a minimal standard of living.

Changes in the poverty rate over time are also affected by the accuracy of the Consumer Price Index. For example, if the Consumer Price Index overstates the rate of increase in the prices of goods and services consumed by low-income households (either because the changes in the prices of these goods change at a different rate from those consumed by middle- and upper-income households, or because improvements in quality of goods and services have not been correctly factored into the consideration of price changes),[1] then the rate of increase in the poverty rate is also overstated. Changes in the Gini coefficient or in the shares of income accruing to each quintile are not affected by changes in or the accuracy of the Consumer Price Index, because this index is not used in their computation.

There are three important differences in the phenomena indicated by the poverty rate and the Gini coefficient that are particularly important in studying changes across metropolitan areas.

1. The income necessary to keep a household above a poverty standard of living is defined for the entire nation; it does not reflect intermetropolitan differences in prices or climate that affect the income necessary to maintain a given living standard.

2. The income level that defines poverty for a given household depends on the age of the persons in the household and the household's size. Children and persons over age 65 require less income to be above the poverty line; larger households require more. Household income distribution measures such as the Gini coefficient and the share by quintile treat a dollar amount accruing to each household the same, regardless of household size or the ages of its members; the designation that a household with a given dollar amount of income is below the poverty level does vary, however, with its size and the ages of it members.

3. While distributional measures such as the Gini coefficient are not dependent on prices and can be sensitive to changes affecting those "in poverty" (i.e., changes in the income accruing to those at the bottom of the distribution), increases in the Gini can also arise from other shifts in the distribution.

Chapter 5 demonstrates that growing MSA inequality in the household income distribution can arise from increases in the share accruing to the top quintile of the MSA at the expense of the third or fourth quintile. For example, changes in earnings inequality decrease the shares accruing to the second through fourth quintiles, increase the share accruing to the top quintile, and have a much smaller but negative effect on the share accruing to the bottom quintile. While MSAs with increases in the proportion of household heads who were African-American had decreases in the share of the middle quintile, and MSAs with increases in the proportion who were over age 65 had increases in the middle quintile shares; the bottom quintile was not affected in MSAs experiencing either of these demographic changes. Shifts in the household income distribution that do not involve changes in the share of income accruing to at least the lower-income households within the bottom quintile cannot affect the poverty rate, since fewer than 20 percent of households are below the poverty level in more than 90 percent of the MSAs studied here.[2] For these reasons, an analysis of whether MSAs with changes in demographic characteristics, in skill composition, in structural or geographic characteristics, and in local labor market vitality had different poverty rates may differ from an analysis of the effects of the same changes on other household inequality measures.

METROPOLITAN CHARACTERISTICS AND POVERTY

To examine, specifically, how changes in characteristics of MSAs are associated with changes in their poverty rates, changes in these characteristics between 1979 and 1989 are regressed on changes in the poverty rate over the same time period. As in Chapter 5's analyses of the Gini coefficient for household income, rates of change rather than absolute levels of poverty are studied because the absolute levels of variables are more likely to be correlated with unobserved differences across metropolitan areas (such as price level differences, for example). Also as in Chapter 5, the analyses are not based on a structural model of urban poverty. Instead, the analyses sort out the *ceteris paribus* correlations between changes in poverty rates for metropolitan areas and changes in their demographic, labor market, skill, and structural characteristics. This exploration, then, begs the question of sorting out endogenous and exogenous variables. While household formation both affects and is affected by local labor market conditions and skill composition, no attempt is made to sort cause from effect. Rather, the emphasis is on sorting out correlations and carefully measuring the interactions between independent variables by estimating a variety of specifications.

Table 7.1 reports the results of regressing percentage changes in MSA characteristics on percentage changes in poverty rates between 1979 and 1989. A negative coefficient for a characteristic indicates that the characteristic is associated with a decrease in the metropolitan poverty rate. Table 7.1 uses the same specifications and formats used in Tables 5.1, 5.4, and 6.2. The first specification, the "basic model," includes changes in demographic and skill compositions and structural characteristics. The second specification, reported in the next column right, adds changes in household formation decisions by earners. The right-most column adds to the second specification the effects of the local labor market and several structural characteristics that are highly correlated with one another and with economic growth. (See Chapter 5 for additional discussion of how to interpret differences in the regression coefficients across specifications.)

Demographic Structure

In the basic model, MSAs experiencing a relative growth in African-American households also experience a relative decrease in their poverty rates, while MSAs with a relative increase in households headed by women experienced an increase in their poverty rates. Once MSA changes in the number of earners in the household are added, however, MSAs that changed the racial composition or the gender composition of their household heads had no significant changes in their poverty rates. Chapter 5 found similar results for racial composition in terms of household income inequality (although MSAs with increases in African-American households had significant decreases in earnings inequality; see Chapter 6), but MSAs with increases in the proportion of households headed by women had significantly greater household income inequality. Because the analysis of MSA quintile shares indicates that this increase in inequality comes from a decrease in the share of the second quintile and an increase in the share of the top quintile, it is not surprising that there is no association with the MSA poverty rate. Households with incomes below the poverty line are almost totally in the bottom quintile, which experienced no significant change in share as the proportion of female-headed households changed (see Table 5.4).

MSAs with more growth in the proportion of households headed by persons over age 65 had greater decreases in their poverty levels, when either earners per household or local labor market conditions and economic growth was controlled. The effects of changes in the proportion of households headed by persons over age 65 are large, negative, and significant for the right-most two columns of Table 7.1. Although still significant, the effects are smaller when controlling for economic growth and labor market conditions, suggesting that high growth MSAs have greater growth in their elderly population.[3] An MSA that increased its proportion of households over age 65 by one standard error had a poverty rate lower by 0.169 standard error. Intermetropolitan variation in the rate of change in the proportion of households over age 65 is one of the most important correlates of intermetropolitan variation in growth in the poverty rate.

The finding that MSAs with growth in elderly households had less growth in poverty rates contrasts with the finding in Chapter 5 that MSAs with changes in this characteristic had no significant change in household income inequality and no change in the share of MSA household income that accrued to the bottom quintile. To the extent that any correlation between household income distribution and the representation of elderly households is found, it is in (statistically insignificantly) increasing shares for the second and third quintiles and decreasing shares for the fourth and fifth quintiles (see Table 6.1). The effect on the share of the bottom quintile is negative, insignificant, and small. The poverty income level for elderly households is lower than for non-elderly households for two reasons: 1) The income necessary for a household to be out of poverty depends on the size of the household, and households headed by the elderly are smaller; and 2) the poverty income level is defined at a lower level for households with elderly heads. Because the elderly composition of MSAs has no effect on the share of income accruing to the bottom fifth of households (which is the quintile that accounts for most of the households with incomes below the poverty level), the negative effect of changes in elderly composition on MSA poverty rates is likely the result of the differing income needs of those households.

Table 7.1 Percentage Changes in Metropolitan Poverty Rates for 181 Metropolitan Areas,[a] 1979–1989[b]

Independent variables	Basic model	Adds earners per hh.	Adds local labor market and growth
Demographic			
Change in % female-headed hh.	0.759	0.195	0.078
	(3.46)	(0.99)	(0.54)
	0.329	0.084	0.034
Change in % no-earner hh.		0.872	0.187
		5.44)	(1.42
		0.649	0.139)
Change in % multiple-earner hh.		−0.353	−0.255
		(−0.96)	0.79
		−0.097	−0.070
Change in % pop. African American	−0.101	−0.054	−0.017
	(−2.41)	(−1.48)	(−0.61)
	−0.191	−0.102	−0.032
Change in % elderly-headed hh.	0.032	−0.497	−.285
	(0.22)	(−3.56)	(−2.74)
	0.019	−0.294	−0.169
Change in %pop. in-migrants			−0.096
			(−1.77)
			−0.085
Change in mean persons per hh.	−0.086	−0.130	−0.219
	(−0.53)	(−0.94)	(−2.06)
	−0.041	−0.062	−0.105
Skill			
Change in median education	−0.436	−0.086	0.264
	(−1.21)	(−0.28)	(1.17)
	−0.085	−0.017	0.051
Change in educational Gini	0.035	0.108	−0.257
	(0.17)	(0.62)	(−1.91)
	0.014	0.042	−0.100
Local labor market			
Change in earnings Gini			1.520
			(4.95)
			0.251
Change in employment-to-population ratio			−0.056
			(−0.16)
			−0.012

Table 7.1 (continued)

Independent variables	Basic model	Adds earners per hh.	Adds local labor market and growth
Other			
Change in ratio of % work/ % live in central city	0.085 (0.98) *0.067*	0.042 (0.57) *0.033*	0.029 (0.53) *0.023*
1980 Population (in 10,000s)	–0.012 (–0.09) *–0.007*	0.128 (1.17) *0.074*	0.131 (1.49) *0.076*
Change in residential segregation index	0.003 (0.95) *0.068*	–0.000 (–0.03) *–0.002*	–0.000 (–0.19) *–0.010*
Change in residents in central city	0.743 (4.08) *0.283*	0.735 (4.76) *0.280*	0.375 (3.23) *0.143*
South Central U.S.A.	0.092 (2.12) *0.179*	0.004 (0.10) *0.007*	–0.026 (–0.89) *–0.051*
Change in mean income			–0.632 (–9.58) *–0.622*
1980 MSA poverty rate	–0.009 (–2.14) *–0.183*	–0.001 (–0.32) *–0.024*	–0.010 (–3.28) *–0.198*
Constant	0.171 (1.79)	0.137 (1.56)	0.830 (8.58)
Adj. R^2	0.22	0.45	0.71

[a] Nassau is eliminated from the poverty analysis because this analysis makes critical use of the central city/MSA differences, and there is no central city in Nassau.
[b] Numbers in parentheses are t-statistics.

The differences in the effects of race, gender, and age of the household head between the basic model and the other specifications arise from the correlation between these demographic characteristics and the household formation decisions of earners. Once we control for earners per household, the negative effect of growth in the proportion of African Americans and the positive effect of growth in female-headed households disappears. Furthermore, the negligible positive effect of growth in elderly households becomes a significant negative effect.

The association between the number of earners in the household and metropolitan poverty rates is as expected. MSAs with increases in the proportion of households with no earners had large increases in poverty, but the proportion of households with no earners appears to reflect metropolitan differences in the overall level of economic opportunity and not differences in labor force participation decisions or household formation patterns among workers. The evidence for this interpretation comes from comparing the coefficients of the proportion of no-earner households in the two right-most columns of Table 7.1. With no controls for growth or labor market, the proportion of no-earner households strongly increases metropolitan poverty, a one-standard-error increase in the proportion of no-earners resulting in a 0.649 increase in the poverty rate. With growth and labor market controls, however, the coefficient of no-earner households is insignificant. The correlation between growth in no-earner households and growth in MSA poverty is fully accounted by differential economic growth and labor market opportunities in those MSAs with greater increases in no-earner households. The regression results that take into account economic growth and labor markets allow us to separate the effects of work choices of households from the effects of the work opportunities they face.[4]

Changes in household size, one of the variables used to define whether household income places the household in poverty, have a statistically insignificant negative correlation with changes in MSA poverty rates in the first two columns of Table 7.1, but a significantly negative effect (also twice as large in size of coefficient) once variables for economic growth and the local labor market are included. These same growth and labor market variables reduce the effects of changes in gender, race, and age compositions of households, variables that are also associated with changes in household size. These results indicate that economic growth is the more important MSA characteristic associated with changes in poverty rates among MSAs, but that once economic growth is considered, MSAs with decreases in household size have higher poverty rates.

MSAs with an increase in the proportion of in-migrants had a decrease in the rate of poverty growth. If the increase in the proportion of in-migrants was one standard error above average, the poverty rate grew at a rate that was 0.085 standard error less than otherwise. As discussed in previous chapters, an increase in in-migration reflects expectations of economic growth, and it is economic growth that reduces the poverty rate.

To summarize, the demographic characteristic that has the strongest association with variation in the poverty rates across MSAs is the MSA proportion of households over age 65. The correlation between decreases in MSA poverty and changes in this characteristic are likely to reflect the fact that poverty incomes for elderly households are set lower than for younger households. MSAs with larger proportions of in-migrants have less poverty. This correlation is due to the correlation of increased in-migration with accelerated growth in economic opportunity. MSAs with growth in economic opportunity reduced their poverty. After controlling for economic growth, however, MSAs with decreases in household size had significantly greater poverty rates. The change in household size is the only demographic shift that has "caused" changes in poverty rates across MSAs.

Skill Composition

Although MSAs with changes in skill composition experienced different changes in the equality of the earnings distribution for professional and management workers, skill composition had no effect on the earnings distribution for other workers or on changes in household income distribution (as analyzed in Chapter 5). For the first two specifications in Table 7.1, neither MSAs with changes in median education nor those with changes in the distribution of education have a different rate of growth in poverty rates. The last column (with controls for local labor market conditions and for economic growth) shows marginal negative significance for the education Gini. An MSA with a rate of increase in the education Gini of one standard error (an increase in educational inequality) had a 0.10 standard error lower poverty rate.

How can an increase in educational inequality decrease poverty? The amount of education was growing dramatically in every MSA between 1980 and 1990. An increase in inequality occurs if those in the middle of the distribution have a smaller overall share of total education in 1990 than they had in 1980. One way this can occur is if those at the lower end or those at the higher end achieved relatively more education. If those at the lower end achieved relatively more, then poverty rates would decrease.

Structural Characteristics

Geographic and structural characteristics of MSAs may also be significantly associated with the rate of change in their poverty levels. Chapter 5 (p. 112) reports that population size (measured by 1980 MSA population) is associated with increasing household income inequality, largely due to increases in the share of the top quintile. When changes in the local labor market and economic growth are added to the analysis, the effect of population decreases but remains positive and significant. The poverty results differ somewhat. Larger MSAs had no significantly different rate of change in poverty, but, when controls for economic growth and local labor market conditions are added, there is a slightly greater tendency for larger MSAs to have more poverty. Larger MSAs do not have different changes in poverty rates than smaller MSAs, but they have more economic growth and, because growth decreases poverty, they should have had less increase in poverty. (Recall from Chapter 6 and Table 6.1 that larger MSAs had a larger increase in earnings inequality.) Because growth in large MSAs does not benefit the poor as much as in smaller MSAs, population size had an insignificantly positive effect on poverty rates in the last column of Table 7.1.

MSAs that had less of a decrease in the proportion of their residents living in the central city experienced significantly greater rates of growth in their poverty levels. About half of the difference appears to arise because MSAs with more population in the central city had slower growth, as evidenced by the lower coefficients in the right-most column: a change in the proportion of MSA residents in the central city that is one standard error above average increases MSA poverty rate growth by 0.143 standard error.

This result is surprising. Metropolitan fragmentation—that is, increasing numbers of municipalities or local governments in a metropolitan area—is expected to worsen poverty by making it easier for the wealthier to separate themselves from the poor. Metropolitan fragmentation increases as the proportion of the population living in the central city decreases. As described in Chapter 2, the separation of richer from poorer results in greater spatial concentration of the poor that in turn may lead to a spatial mismatch between where the poor live and where the jobs are, and also to neighborhoods that offer inferior opportunities for the poor to obtain human capital in the form of information and skills (Cutler and Glaeser 1997). Both of these effects of decreases in the proportion of the population residing in the central city are expected to lead to increases in MSA poverty rates.

The quintile analysis in Chapter 5 shows that decreases in the proportion of the MSA population residing in the central city increased the share of the bottom three quintiles at the expense of the top two quintiles, with the largest effects occurring in quintiles two and five. The quintile results can be reconciled with the poverty rate results in two ways.

1) The positive effect on income share for the bottom quintile may be attributed to the second decile, with the first decile (where most poverty households are counted) experiencing the opposite relationship. The fact that the bottom quintile shows less of a positive effect than the second quintile in Table 5.4 suggests that the positive effect of larger central cities on income shares decreases at the lower levels of income.

2) The differences between the households included in the bottom quintile and the households included in the group with incomes below the poverty level, which are defined with respect to age and household size but ignoring MSA price levels, account for the differences. The MSAs that have less of a decrease (or an increase) in the proportion of residents living in the central city are different with respect to other attributes that are associated with poverty rates but not with household income shares. MSAs in California and Florida[5] dominate the outlying increas-

ers and decreasers in central city population. Because the two coasts generally experienced greater economic growth, their changes in poverty rates (a measure that depends on income level, as opposed to income distributional measures like the Gini coefficient and shares of income to quintiles that do not) may lead to different results.

Consistent with the results reported in Chapter 5 for both the household income Gini coefficient and the shares accruing to quintiles, an increase in the proportion of jobs in the central city relative to the proportion of residents in the city (a measure of the spatial match between jobs and center city residents) has a positive but statistically insignificant effect on the growth in MSA poverty.

Changes in the extent of racial segregation in housing have no effect on changes in the MSA poverty rate. South Central[6] MSAs have a marginally significant greater increase in their poverty rates in the basic model. When earners and labor market/growth variables are considered, the South Central has a statistically insignificant and smaller rate of increase in poverty rates between 1979 and 1989. Obviously, MSAs with greater income growth have less growth in their poverty rates. As expected,[7] MSAs with higher poverty rates in 1979 tend to have slower rates of growth in poverty, after considering variations in local economic conditions.

Local Labor Market Characteristics

Not surprisingly, the structure of the local labor market influences variations in metropolitan poverty rates. An increase of one standard error in the change in the earnings Gini coefficient in an MSA is associated with an increase of 0.251 standard error in the change in the metropolitan poverty rate between 1979 and 1989.

MSAs with tightening of the labor markets, as represented by increases in the employment-to-population ratio, do not have significantly greater changes in their poverty rates, however, after controlling for changes in the number of earners per household. Because the lack of earners in a household contributes to growth of poverty, MSAs with more equal distribution of wages or jobs have less poverty.

SUMMARY

Economic growth and local labor market conditions influence the growth of poverty in MSAs. Based on the beta coefficients from the right-most column of Table 7.1, the most important variable is the growth in mean per-capita income. Because the poverty rate is defined with respect to income levels, this is not at all surprising. The next variables, in order of importance, are increases in the earnings Gini, higher 1980 MSA poverty rates, increases in households over age 65 (reflecting that such households require less income to be above the poverty index), changes in the proportion of MSA residents in the central city, and increases in the proportion of households without an earner.

The principal findings are that

- MSAs with more economic growth have less poverty; this effect is stronger for smaller MSAs.

- MSA labor markets that offer a more unequal distribution of wage and salary opportunities have higher poverty rates.

- MSAs with increases in the proportion of the population that is African American or in the proportion of households headed by unmarried women had no different growth in their poverty rates, once local economic conditions are considered.

- MSAs with increases in the proportion of households headed by a person over age 65 had greater decreases in their poverty rates.

- Increasing income and racial segmentation within the MSA did not significantly affect MSA poverty rates.

Notes

1. See Boskin and Jorgenson (1997).
2. In 1990, the only MSAs in this study that had poverty rates in excess of 20 percent were Fresno, CA (21.4); Visalia, CA (22.6); Gainesville, FL (22.7); Alexandria, LA (22.6); Lafayette, LA (21.7); New Orleans, LA (21.2); Shreveport, LA (22.0); Brownsville, TX (39.7); Corpus Christi, TX (21.3); El Paso, TX (26.8); McAllen, TX (41.9); Waco, TX (20.6); Yakima, WA (20.2); and Huntington, WV (20.3).
3. Presumably, this difference reflects the migration patterns of retired workers.

4. When number-of-earners-per-household variables are removed while the employ-ment-to-population variable is included, the effects of race and gender composi-tion of households become significant. This result arises because MSAs with more African-American and/or female-headed households have more poverty because such households have fewer earners, *ceteris paribus*.

5. The average MSA decreased this proportion (see Table 4.4). The largest rates of decrease in the proportion living in the central city after Atlanta (–28 percent) were Sarasota, FL (–24 percent), Daytona Beach, FL (–24 percent), Lawrence, MA (–21 percent), West Palm Beach, FL (–20 percent), Riverside, CA (–20 per-cent), Tampa, FL (–19 percent), Richmond, VA (–19 percent), Augusta, GA (–18 percent), Fort Lauderdale, FL (–18 percent), Atlantic City, NJ (–18 percent), and Bremerton, WA (–18 percent). The largest rates of increase after Chico, CA (17 percent) were Bakersfield, CA (15 percent), Melbourne, FL (14 percent), Visalia, CA (13 percent), and Fall River, MA (13 percent).

6. "South Central" includes the East South Central and the West South Central states: Kentucky, Tennessee, Alabama, Mississippi, Arkansas, Louisiana, Okla-homa, and Texas.

7. The 1980 level acts as a "standardization" for the percentage change. The negative effect means that there is regression to the mean in the sense that MSAs with larger poverty rates grew less, i.e., approaching the mean, and those with smaller poverty rates grew more, also approaching the mean.

8 The Concentration of Poverty in the Central City

The association between MSA characteristics and the distribution of poverty between city and suburb (i.e., the extent of the concentration of metropolitan poverty in the central city) may differ from their association with the overall poverty rate for the metropolis. In general, MSAs that are more segregated by income are expected, of course, to have more of their poor in one place and therefore to have higher concentrations of poverty in the central city. Those MSA characteristics that are associated with greater residential segmentation are expected, therefore, to result in greater concentrations of poverty in the central city. MSAs with greater growth in residential segregation by race, with more African Americans, or with fewer in-migrants are expected to have higher concentrations of poverty in the central city.

Based on an analysis of changes in the proportion of MSA poverty that is in the central city in the 1980s, the analysis presented in this chapter finds that

- metropolitan area poverty is becoming increasingly concentrated in the central cities, and the rate of concentration is accelerating in those MSAs with the highest levels of concentration;

- economic growth, which was shown in the previous chapters to decrease metropolitan poverty and household income inequality, has little effect on the distribution of poverty between city and suburb;

- the racial composition of the metropolitan area, which was shown in the previous chapter to have little influence on metropolitan poverty, had slightly greater influence on the extent to which that poverty concentrates in the central city;

- metropolitan areas with more of their population residing in the central city are shown to have higher overall poverty rates, but this chapter finds that there is less of a differential between the amounts of poverty in the city and the suburbs for MSAs with larger central cities;

- movement of jobs from the city to the suburbs has little relationship with metropolitan poverty rates or the concentration of MSA poverty in the central city; and

- an increase in earnings inequality in the metropolitan area is associated with increased poverty, but it is also associated with a more even distribution of that poverty between city and suburb.

METROPOLITAN CHARACTERISTICS AND THE CONCENTRATION OF POVERTY

We examine the tendency of poverty to concentrate in the central city of the MSA by measuring the rate of change in the proportion of total MSA poverty that is in the central city. Because MSAs vary in the size of the central city relative to the overall MSA, I measure the percentage change in that ratio during the 1980s, while controlling for changes in the boundaries of the MSA and of the central city. Table 8.1 reports the association between changes in the concentration of metropolitan poverty in the central city and changes in MSA characteristics.

Demographic Structure

MSAs with different demographic structures experience systematically different changes in the concentration of poverty in their central cities, and demographic structure has systematically different associations with concentration than it has with the overall MSA change in poverty.

While MSAs with increases in their African-American populations had insignificantly less poverty growth (see Table 7.1), these MSAs had an increase in the concentration of poverty in the central city (Table 8.1), although the effect is of marginal statistical significance. MSAs with increases in female-headed households, changes in the distribution of wage earners across MSA households, and changes in MSA household size had no differential increases in the concentration of poverty over the decade. (It is interesting to note that changes in household size had a positive, but insignificant, effect on changes in the concentration of poverty, presumably arising because larger households are less likely to be poor and less likely to reside in the central city.) MSAs that increase their proportion of households over 65 experience a deconcentration of poverty from the central city. The elderly population is less likely to be poor and more likely to reside in the city than is the younger population.

Skill Composition

The analyses reported in Chapters 5 and 7 show that measures of MSA skill composition have no significant effect on their household income inequality or poverty rates. Changes in median education have no significant influence on changes in the concentration of poverty in the central city, but changes in the distribution of education are associated with central city poverty. MSAs with more unequal distributions of education (as measured by an increase in the Gini) had poverty more concentrated in their central cities. An MSA with a change in its education Gini that is one standard error above the mean had an increase in the concentration of poverty that was between 0.22 and 0.25 standard error above the mean (Table 8.1). The coefficient of the education Gini increased when controls for the effects of the education distribution on labor market outcomes (as measured by the employment-to-population ratio, the earnings distribution, and other variables correlated with economic expansion) were added.

These results indicate that the distribution of education affects the concentration of poverty by affecting household residential location patterns. MSAs that became more educationally unequal were more likely to have selective migration of nonpoor, more educated persons from the city to the suburbs.

Structural Characteristics

Geographic and other structural characteristics of MSAs are also significantly associated with the extent to which poverty is concentrated in the central city. As with the growth in MSA poverty, the growth in the concentration of poverty is strongly influenced by the proportion of MSA residents in the central city: increases in this proportion strongly decreased the rate of concentration of poverty in the central city. An increase that was one standard error above the mean

**Table 8.1 Percentage Changes in the Ratio of Central City to MSA
Poverty Rates for 181 Metropolitan Areas,[a] 1979–1989[b]**

Independent variable	Basic model	Adds earners per hh.	Adds local labor market and growth
Demographic			
Change in % female-headed hh.	−0.008	−0.004	0.045
	(−0.09)	(−0.05)	(0.50)
	−0.008	*−0.004*	*0.044*
Change in % no-earner hh.		−0.027	0.010
		(−0.37)	(0.13)
		−0.045	*0.017*
Change in % multiple-earner hh.		−0.072	−0.223
		(−0.42)	(−1.09)
		−0.045	*−0.139*
Change in % pop. African American	0.034	0.033	0.029
	(2.07)	(1.91)	(1.63)
	0.146	*0.139*	*0.122*
Change in % elderly-headed hh.	−0.111	−0.106	−0.104
	(−0.92)	(−1.62)	(−1.61)
	−0.148	*−0.141*	*−0.139*
Change in % in-migrant hh.			0.023
			(0.65)
			0.045
Change in mean persons per hh.	0.032	0.028	0.033
	(0.48)	(0.43)	(0.49)
	0.034	*0.030*	*0.035*
Skill			
Change in mean education	0.026	0.025	0.063
	(0.19)	(0.17)	(0.44)
	0.012	*0.011*	*0.028*
Change in education Gini	0.249	0.252	0.288
	(3.21)	(3.22)	(3.65)
	0.218	*0.221*	*0.252*
Local labor market			
Change in earnings Gini			−0.706
			(−3.68)
			−0.263

Table 8.1 (continued)

Independent variable	Basic model	Adds earners per hh.	Adds local labor market and growth
Change in employment-to-population ratio			0.184 (0.87) *0.086*
Other			
Change in ratio of % work/% live in central city	−0.053 (−1.53) *−0.095*	−0.055 (−1.54) *−0.098*	−0.045 (−1.27) *−0.080*
Change in population			−0.29 (−0.54) *−0.050*
Population in 1980 (in 10,000s)	−0.144 (−2.76) *−0.188*	−0.145 (−2.74) *−0.189*	−0.079 (−1.42) *−0.103*
Change in residential segregation index	0.002 (1.74) *0.116*	0.002 (1.73) *0.117*	0.002 (1.42 *0.103*
Change in residents in central city	−0.473 (−6.07) *−0.406*	−0.477 (−6.04) *−0.410*	−0.463 (−5.81) *−0.400*
South Central U.S.A.	0.005 (0.32) *0.023*	0.003 (0.18) *0.014*	0.015 (0.85) *0.066*
1980 ratio of central city to MSA poverty rate	0.033 (1.94) *0.152*	0.032 (1.91) *0.151*	0.025 (1.44) *0.118*
Change in central city area	−0.000 (−1.50) *−0.096*	−0.000 (−1.54) *−0.100*	−0.000 (−1.53) *−0.110*
MSA missing index	−0.017 (−0.45) *−0.028*	−0.017 (−0.45) *−0.029*	−0.043 (−1.02) *−0.072*
Constant	−0.012 (−0.32)	−0.006 (−0.15)	−0.012 (−0.24)
Adj. R^2	0.37	0.36	0.41

[a] Nassau is eliminated from the poverty analysis because this analysis makes critical use of the central city/MSA differences and there is no central city in Nassau.

[b] Numbers in parentheses are *t*-statistics.

decreased the rate of concentration of poverty by 0.40 to 0.41 standard error. Because this variable had an opposite effect on MSA poverty, however, this represents a rearrangement of poverty from the city to the suburbs in a way that actually increases overall MSA poverty.

MSAs with increases in the ratio of the proportion of their jobs to the proportion of their residents in the central city had less growth (statistically insignificant) in the concentration of poverty (and insignificant increases in overall poverty also). The results presented here do not offer much optimism that a relocation of employment within the metropolitan area can reduce overall poverty or be a promising solution to the increase in its concentration.

Central cities that expanded their boundaries through annexation (Table 8.1, "Change in central city area") had less poverty (but generally at a statistically insignificant level), presumably because annexed areas had less poverty than the rest of the central city.[1] MSAs in which poverty was more concentrated in the central cities in 1979 experienced increased concentrations of poverty into the central cities between 1979 and 1989. MSAs with a concentration of poverty in the central city that was one standard error above average in 1979 experienced growth in the central city poverty concentration between 0.12 and 0.15 standard error above the average growth. These results suggest an acceleration of the concentration of metropolitan poverty in the MSAs with greater concentration rates.

Neither growth in mean income nor population (which were both significant in decreasing MSA poverty) were significantly associated with the concentration of poverty in the city (data not shown). While economic growth was clearly associated with a decrease in MSA poverty, it had no relationship to the distribution of that poverty between city and suburbs.

Local Labor Market Characteristics

Surprisingly, MSAs with increases in the inequality of the earnings distribution (which were associated with increases in overall MSA poverty) experienced decreases in the concentration of poverty in their central cities between 1979 and 1989, at a statistically significant level. These results hold for the model reported in the third column and also when the variables correlated with economic expansion are excluded (not shown).

One possible explanation of this result is that MSAs with more earnings equality have more persons earning middle-level incomes— recall that Table 5.4 showed that decreases in earnings inequality increased the shares of the second and third quintiles and reduced the share of the top quintile of households.   Middle-level-income house-holds may have been more likely than those with high incomes to move to the suburbs during the 1980s. If this were the case, MSAs with an increase in middle-income persons would experience a rela-tively greater tendency to concentrate low-income persons in central cities.

Continuing the surprising local labor market results, MSAs with increasing tightness of the labor market (higher employment-to-popula-tion ratios) experienced insignificant increases in the concentration of poverty in their central cities; the explanation for this is the same as for the effects of rising earnings inequality, i.e., greater effects on the shares accruing to the second and third quintiles than on the lowest quintile. The issue here is one of location within the MSA.   As with earnings inequality, if increases in the employment-to-population ratio disproportionately benefit middle-income households (which are more likely to move to the suburbs), then the concentration of poverty increases. These results suggest that employment-to-population ratios rise by expanding the employment of middle-income suburban resi-dents (i.e., dependent spouses and children of higher earners) or city residents who then move to the suburbs, rather than members of lower-income city households.

The beta coefficients reported in the last column of Table 8.1 sum-marize the relative importance of changes in MSA demographics, MSA skill composition, other characteristics, and the local labor market on changes in the concentration of metropolitan poverty in central cities. In order of importance, the characteristics most strongly influencing increases in the concentration of MSA poverty in central cities are changes in the proportion of residents in the central city (−0.400); the MSA wage and salary Gini coefficient (−0.263), the MSA educational Gini coefficient (0.252), proportion of the MSA population over age 65 (−0.139), proportion of households with multiple earners (−0.139), pro-portion of the MSA population African American (0.122), 1980 ratio of

central city to MSA poverty (0.118), change in the central city boundaries (–0.110), and increases in residential segregation by race (0.103).

SUMMARY

Several factors account for intermetropolitan variations in the concentration of poverty in central cities. The principal findings are that

- MSA poverty has become increasingly concentrated in the central cities, and the rate of increase appears to be greater for those
  MSAs with the greatest concentration.

- Although MSAs with more economic growth had less poverty,
  these MSAs have no different distribution of poverty between
  their city and suburbs.

- Although MSA labor markets that offer a more unequal distribution of earnings opportunities had higher poverty rates, the poverty is more evenly distributed between suburbs and the central
  city.

- MSAs with increases in the proportion of African-American
  households and households with the head under age 65 have
  greater concentrations of poverty in the central city.

- Increasing the proportion of MSA jobs in the central city was
  associated with increases in MSA overall poverty and had no significant effect on central city poverty.

Note

1. Arguably, annexation is correlated with economic growth and might have been
    included only in Column 3 of Table 8.1. The inclusion or exclusion of the annex-
    ation variable affected only the third digit of the coefficient of the other indepen-
    dent variables, changing no signs or statistical significance.

9 The Role of the Macro-Environment in Poverty and Household Income Inequality

The results detailed in Chapters 5 through 8 show that changes in MSA demographic structure and in employment, as well as changes in earnings inequality, are strongly associated with the rising household income inequality and poverty rates described in Chapter 1.

Rising earnings inequality does not translate directly into rising household income inequality. If, as was the case for some MSAs, the rise in earnings inequality occurs with an expansion of employment, the net effect of these two labor market trends may actually reduce household income inequality. When earnings inequality increases because persons who previously had no earnings income (and who thus were not previously included in the measurement of earnings inequality) become "low earners," public policymakers need not be concerned. If household income inequality is decreasing, then rising earnings inequality is less likely to be a problem.

Other characteristics of MSAs were less useful in distinguishing MSAs with greater increases in inequality or poverty from those with less. Neither changes in the MSA average level of education nor in the relative inequality of the distribution of education among MSA residents are correlated with differences in household income distribution within MSAs. Structural characteristics of MSAs—such as in the size of the central city relative to the suburbs, the extent of residential segregation by race, and the density of jobs relative to residents in the central city—have little or no connection to changes in household income inequality. Larger MSAs tended to have more income inequality and poverty, however. Changes in skills and in metropolitan structure did not seem to influence or be influenced by household income inequality and poverty.

SUMMARY OF THE RESULTS

Assume, for the sake of discussion, that we know that the measured correlations between MSA characteristics and their poverty or income inequality rates reflect causation; that is, the changes in the characteristics of MSAs caused the changes in poverty or income inequality. Given this assumption, Table 9.1 lists the estimated average contribution of the various metropolitan characteristics analyzed on the amount of growth in the household income Gini, the poverty rate, and the ratio of the central city to the MSA poverty rate. The estimated contributions reported on Table 9.1 represent the multiplication of the mean values of the characteristics (reported in Table 3.3) by the regression coefficients reported in the right-most columns of Table 5.1 (for the household income Gini), Table 7.1 (for the poverty rate), and Table 8.1 (for the ratio of central city to MSA poverty rates).

Demographic Structure

There is evidence that MSAs that experienced greater decreases in average household size had significantly greater increases in inequality and poverty rates.[1] MSAs experiencing greater growth in the proportion of households headed by unmarried women and of households without earners had significantly greater increases in inequality. MSAs with an aging population (i.e., those with increases in the proportion of households headed by persons over age 65) experienced relative decreases in their poverty rate. The racial composition of MSAs was not associated with their poverty rates or the extent of income inequality.

The demographic choices that Americans make about the households in which they live vary across MSAs, and these MSA differences are associated with the MSA's levels of income inequality and poverty. Whether public policy should or could be used to alter the differences in MSA demographic structure that are associated with rising inequality or poverty of metropolitan areas is not at all clear. First, these MSA shifts in household structures may be the result of poverty or inequality, not the cause. Second, even if the demographic differences do cause the changes in poverty and inequality, the changes in family or household circumstances may make individuals better off, in spite of

**Table 9.1 Major Factors in Growth in Metropolitan Poverty and
Income Inequality**

Variable	Household income Gini (%)	Poverty rate (%)	Ratio of central city to MSA poverty rates (%)
Total increase 1979–1989	10.6	9.4	8.0
Estimated contribution of demographic changes			
Female-headed proportion	1.6***	1.2	0.7
No-earner proportion	0.4*	1.4	0.1
Multi-earner proportion	0.7	−1.7	−1.5
African-American proportion	−0.1	−0.5	5.9*
Elderly-headed proportion	−0.9	−14.7***	−0.9
In-migrant proportion	0.0	0.0	0.0
Household size	3.6***	3.2**	−0.5
Estimated contribution of education changes			
Mean education	−0.2	2.7	0.6
Gini education coefficient	0.4	−6.4*	7.2***
Estimated contribution of structural changes			
Ratio of % work/% live in central city	0.0	0.1	−0.1
Population	−1.6	−0.8	−0.6
Residential segregation index	0.0	0.2	0.0
Residents in central city	0.2	−1.9***	2.4***
Per-capita income	0.2	−58.8***	0.9
1980 Level of dependent variable	−24.4***	−11.4***	3.5
1980 Population	0.5***	1.1	−0.6
Estimated contribution of local labor market			
Earnings Gini	1.5***	4.2***	−2.0***
Employment/population ratio	−2.3***	−0.4	1.3

*Computed based on coefficient that was statistically significant at $p > 0.10$.
**Computed based on coefficient that was statistically significant at $p > 0.05$.
***Computed based on coefficient that was statistically significant at $p > 0.01$.

their income implications, than other options which reduce poverty and inequality by having individuals live in less-preferred household circumstances.

The clearest public policy implication of the importance of changing family and household structures is that demographic choices may undermine the efficacy of other strategies aimed at reducing poverty or income inequality within an MSA. That portion of poverty and household income inequality that arises from changes in household formation patterns will not be changed by public policies that alter labor demand, skills, or geographical/political structures but do not alter preferences for household or family composition. To the extent that additional policy responses aimed at that portion of inequality or poverty that arises from demographic choices are needed, the greatest consensus will be on those policies directed at persons who have not chosen their household—i.e., the children—to improve their well-being and increase their opportunities to acquire skills.

Although MSA changes in racial composition had no relationship to changes in the income distribution or the extent of poverty within an MSA, racial changes were associated with changes in the location of poverty in MSAs. MSAs with more African Americans had no more poverty than others but were more likely to concentrate that poverty in their central cities.

Although African Americans are more likely to be poor than other Americans, MSAs with greater growth in the African-American population did not experience either more poverty or more income inequality. This result is consistent with race affecting who is poor (the distribution of income and opportunity) but not the extent of poverty or inequality. The result is also consistent with attributing current racial differences in income to labor market discrimination, because racial composition has no apparent effect on the overall productive capacity (to the extent that productivity variation across MSAs is indexed by the poverty rate or income level) of the MSA,[2] but it does affect who is receiving the lower incomes in the MSA. Similarly, the fact that racial composition does affect whether MSA poverty is concentrated in the central city is consistent with housing discrimination against African Americans.

Skill Composition

MSAs with greater changes in the skill composition of their population did not experience different changes in poverty or income inequality, nor was there any change in the extent to which their poverty was concentrated in the central city. While the results reported in Table 9.1 are based on an analysis that holds changes in the equality of the earnings distribution constant, increases in median education were not significant when the local earnings Ginis were not included (see Tables 5.1 and 7.1) nor were they significant in the analysis of earnings inequality (see Table 6.1).

Research based on the national economy has clearly demonstrated that education plays a critical role in changing inequality of earnings over time because education has become more valuable in the labor market, increasing the wages of those that have it and decreasing the wages of those who do not. The research also demonstrates that the increasing return on education is the result of demographic or labor supply changes that have resulted in a proportional decrease in highly educated workers entering the market and is also the result of labor demand changes that have made skill more valuable in production.

Yet, these phenomena do not lead to a statistically significant coefficient for changes in the average education level within a local labor market. The effects of increases in average educational attainment on local income inequality depend on how evenly education has increased across the population. If the increase occurs because a larger proportion of the population moves into higher levels of education, then overall income inequality is expected to decrease. In this case, there is an increase in supply of persons with "high end" skills and wages, reducing the equilibrium wage for the more highly skilled. If the increase in education is evenly distributed, there may well be no effects on income inequality.

The more telling variable, then, is changes in the Gini coefficient for the distribution of educational attainment among adults. The association of increasing educational inequality with increases in household income inequality was positive but statistically insignificant; increasing educational inequality contributed to decreases in the poverty rate and was positively associated with the concentration of MSA poverty in the central city. The quintile analyses showed a decrease in the share of income accruing to the top quintile and an increase in share to all other quintiles (especially those in the middle) as the Gini coefficient for education increased. The inclusion or exclusion of local labor market characteristics had no effect on these outcomes.

In the end, metropolitan areas with increases in educational inequality experienced no statistically significant changes in income inequality relative to MSAs without such increases. An important reason is that, relatively, there was not much cross-sectional variability in changes in educational inequality. Table 3.3 shows a standard deviation for the change in the education Gini that is small (7.6) relative to the mean change in the Gini (25 percent). Similarly, the standard deviation of the percentage change in median education (3.8) is small relative to the percentage change in education (10.1). The changes in education and its distribution are relatively larger over longer time periods in the national data than they are in this cross section of MSAs in the 1980s.

The relative unimportance of MSA changes in educational attainment or its distribution in terms of MSA changes in household income inequality arise, then, from two sources. The first is that the increases in educational attainment inequality across MSAs in the 1980s appear to have arisen from increases in the proportion of the population with the highest levels of education, which tended to increase supply relative to demand for the more highly skilled, reducing their relative earnings and increasing income equality. The second is that there was not sufficient variation in changes in educational equality relative to changes in income inequality to provide as powerful a statistical test of the relationships as is the case in longer-duration national data.

Structural Characteristics

The geographic structure of metropolitan areas was only modestly associated with the changes they experienced in income inequality and poverty rates. MSAs that became more racially segregated did not have significantly greater growth in poverty or overall household income inequality. MSAs with growing segregation did decrease the share of income accruing to the top quintile while increasing the share of quintiles 2 and 3, however. This effect is consistent with segregation having social costs in the sense of decreasing efficiency, that is, decreasing the quality of the match between workers and jobs. Segregation may reduce competition from quintile-1 households for jobs typically taken by members of quintile-2 and quintile-3 households, increasing the earnings of quintiles 2 and 3 while decreasing that of quintile 1. Segregation may reduce the productivity and profitability of MSA businesses, contributing to a reduction in the share of quintile 5.

Larger MSAs had significantly greater growth in inequality and insignificantly greater growth in poverty (see Tables 5.1 and 7.1). The income inequality effect is greatest when local labor market characteristics are not included, but remains significant (although half the size) even with controls for employment and earnings inequality.

Larger MSAs have more earnings inequality. This result is consistent with the hypothesis that technology or productivity changes and intensity of competition account for increases in inequality. Larger MSAs allow a finer articulation of skill and tighter matches between job requirements and worker skills. Earnings, then, are more tightly tied to skill and more reflective of marginal product, more set by the "market" and less set by "institutions." Yet half of the effect of MSA size remains after controlling for these labor market characteristics. Larger MSAs are more "anonymous" and have a greater range of households, as indicated by their tendency to have more female-headed households. These social "nonconformity" effects associated with size also contribute to income inequality and poverty.

The strongest evidence on the relationship between structure and poverty or income inequality is with respect to the size of the central city and the location of employment. MSAs whose central cities account for more of the MSA population have greater poverty, but it is less concentrated in the central city. While the latter result may be a simple artifact of the central city including more of the MSA population, the difference in concentration affects the fiscal capacity of local government to address poverty problems.

No relationship between the ratio of jobs to residents in the central city and poverty or income inequality was evident, suggesting that the sorting of employment between cities and suburbs is simply not relevant. This study, then, finds no support for the hypothesis that job access and spatial mismatch contribute to MSA inequality or to MSA poverty rates. The effect of the ratio of jobs to residents also was not evident even for the concentration of poverty in the central city (the sign was as expected, but the coefficient was not significant). The lack of statistical significance for this variable does not arise from any lack of variability in the data set, as was argued above for the educational measures. Table 3.3 shows that the ratio had a mean of 3.15 and a standard deviation of 15.5.

For both MSA changes in poverty rates and in income inequality, there was a tendency to "regress to the mean," in that MSAs with higher rates of income inequality, with quintiles with higher shares of income, or with higher rates of poverty, experienced less growth in these variables. This may reflect a tendency for the system to "self-correct" or it may be an artifact of measurement error.[3] It is, therefore, quite surprising that the "regression to the mean" effect is not observed in the concentration of MSA poverty in central cities. In this case, MSAs with disproportionate shares of poverty in their central cities did not tend to have less growth in the concentration, they had more (albeit at a statistically insignificant rate). This suggests that the concentration of poverty feeds on itself, in the sense that MSAs with more concentration continue to increase their concentration at a faster rate.

Local Labor Market

Clearly, the local labor market matters, but as we have noted throughout the study, there is not a perfect translation of earnings inequality into household income inequality. MSAs with a 10 percent increase in their earnings Gini coefficient averaged a 5 percent increase in their household income inequality. Earnings inequality does not translate perfectly into household income inequality because households have varying numbers of earners and changes in the distribution of earners over households counters the growth in earnings inequality.

To compare the effects of changes in the earnings Gini with the effects of changes in the employment-to-population ratio or to examine the effects of either labor market measure on quintile shares or on the poverty rate, the standardized beta coefficients are more informative. A 1.0-standard-error increase in MSA earnings inequality is associated with a 0.37-standard-error increase in MSA household income inequality (see Table 5.1) and a 0.25- to 0.30-standard-error increase in MSA poverty rates (see Table 7.1). The changes occur primarily at the middle and the top end of the distribution of household income, however, with a decrease of 0.41 standard error in the share of MSA income accruing to the middle (third) quintile, an increase of 0.38 standard error for the top quintile, and no significant difference in share for the bottom quintile (see Table 5.4).

The MSA employment-to-population ratio is more consistently related to the household income distribution. There is a strong positive relationship to the share of MSA income accruing to the bottom three quintiles (with the largest effects for the bottom two quintiles) and a negative effect on the share of the top two quintiles (with the larger negative effect at the highest quintile).[4] This redistribution among the quintiles means that a 1 percent increase in the employment-to-population ratio was associated with a 0.034 percent decrease in the metropolitan household income Gini (see Table 5.1).

Table 9.1 shows that, although rising inequality in earnings was associated with increasing rates of household income inequality in MSAs, the increases in the employment-to-population ratio had a larger correlation in the opposite direction. Recall that Chapter 1 contended that it was necessary to study household income inequality (which includes all persons) rather than earnings inequality (which includes only persons with wages) to judge the total distributional effects (wages and employment) of changes in earnings inequality. Overall, changes in the metropolitan labor markets are associated with decreases in household income inequality. The increases in employment, on average, offset the effects of rising earnings inequality.

Although MSAs with employment-to-population increases reduced their poverty rates, the result is not statistically significant. Because the categorization of whether a household has income that places it below the poverty level is based on household composition as well as on the income level, the differences in the association of changes in the employment-to-population ratio with household income inequality and with the poverty rate arises from the effects of shifting household demography.

POLICY CONCLUSIONS

These results strongly support the widely held view that metropolitan economic growth reduces metropolitan poverty.[5] Therefore, all policies designed to promote growth in jobs are antipoverty policies. Similarly, household income inequality is substantially reduced by tightening of labor markets.

Furthermore, the evidence presented here suggests that it does not matter where in the metropolitan area—city or suburbs—that job growth occurs: the intrametropolitan location of jobs had no significant effect on overall MSA poverty rates or household income inequality. When MSA jobs were more concentrated in the central city, however, poverty was insignificantly less concentrated in the central city.

Policies which create more jobs, regardless of wage level, lower household income inequality and MSA poverty rates. The evidence in this study indicates that the creation of low-wage jobs (which provide wages to those who previously had none) may increase earnings inequality, but it reduces income inequality, which is the more important measure of well-being.

The type of jobs that are added as economic growth occurs does matter, however. Adding middle-income jobs (rather than jobs at the high or low end of the wage distribution) decreases overall MSA poverty and reduces household income inequality more. However, more middle-income jobs contribute to a greater concentration of poverty in the central city, probably because middle-income earners and households with a single earner whose income puts them over the poverty level are more likely to live in the suburbs.

Finally, the significant association between African-American representation in the MSA and the concentration of poverty in the central city, coupled with the finding that there is no relationship between race and overall MSA poverty, indicates the importance of antidiscrimination policies in housing and in the labor market for improving the income status of African Americans.

Notes

1.   Although there is some concern about how much weight should be attached to this result given the sensitivity to the way income distribution is measured, there

are no significant effects of household size when absolute differences in income shares to households by quintiles are analyzed in Chapter 5.

2. In general, economists believe that wages, at least in the aggregate, reflect the productivity of workers. If wages reflect productivity and if wages are correlated with income and poverty rates, then productivity variation across MSAs would be correlated with, or indexed by, the poverty rate.

3. A measurement error correction occurs when the "extreme" values are mismeasured so that in the next period the value is corrected.

4. Table 5.4 shows that a one-standard-error increase in the employment-to-population ratio is associated with an increase of 0.33, 0.34, and 0.25 standard error in the share of income accruing to quintiles 1, 2, and 3, respectively. A 1.0-standard-error increase in the employment-to-population ratio is associated with a decrease of 0.25 and 0.30 standard error in the share of income accruing to quintiles 4 and 5.

5. The large coefficients on percentage changes in proportions of in-migrants and in proportions of households with no earners and with multiple earners in Table 7.1 provide evidence of the role of economic growth. Because the coefficients on number of earners in the household were not significant when economic growth measures are added in the right-most column of that table, the results point to the role of job availability in reducing poverty.

Appendix

Supplementary Tables

Table A.1 Correlations between MSA Characteristics

Decennial rates of change in	Living in central city	Proportion African-American	Different MSA 5 years ago	% Jobs/% residents in central city	Hholds headed by over age 65	Hholds headed by lone woman	Hholds with no earner	Hholds with multi earners
Living in central city	1.00	0.11	-0.13	-0.17	0.09	0.14	0.05	-0.09
Proportion African-American	0.11	1.00	-0.04	0.05	-0.13	0.22	-0.11	0.02
Different MSA 5 years ago	-0.13	-0.04	1.00	-0.09	-0.10	-0.27	-0.19	0.27
% Jobs/% residents in central city	-0.17	0.05	-0.09	1.00	-0.09	-0.07	-0.04	-0.06
Hholds headed by over age 65	0.09	-0.13	-0.10	-0.09	1.00	0.53	0.65	-0.45
Hholds headed by woman	0.14	0.22	-0.27	-0.07	0.53	1.00	0.53	-0.45
Households with no earner	0.05	-0.11	-0.19	-0.04	0.65	0.53	1.00	-0.78
Hholds with multi earners	-0.09	0.02	0.27	-0.06	-0.45	-0.45	-0.78	1.00
Hhold size	0.01	-0.34	-0.06	-0.04	-0.13	-0.10	-0.07	-0.01
Gini coeff on ed	0.00	0.06	0.06	-0.02	-0.01	0.12	0.04	0.10
Median ed, 25–64 yrs. old	-0.11	-0.11	-0.02	0.09	-0.10	0.00	-0.17	0.11
Employ/pop, 25–64 yr. olds	-0.13	-0.07	0.20	0.00	-0.31	-0.39	-0.51	0.74
Per capita income	-0.15	0.09	0.37	0.05	-0.29	-0.31	-0.62	0.54
Gini coeff on earnings	-0.01	-0.24	-0.18	0.10	0.29	0.23	0.42	-0.38
Gini coeff on hhold income	0.01	0.11	-0.01	0.02	0.43	0.42	0.54	-0.36
1980 Gini coeff hhold income	-0.08	-0.13	-0.17	0.07	-0.18	-0.03	-0.23	-0.08
Residential segregation index	-0.04	0.09	0.17	-0.15	0.14	-0.05	0.14	-0.04

Table A.1 (continued)

Decennial rates of change in	Hhold size	Gini coeff on educ.	Median educ. for 25–64 yrs. old	Employ/pop. for 25–64 yrs. old	Per capita income	Gini coeff on earnings	Gini coeff on hhold income	1980 Gini coeff on hhold income
Living in central city	0.01	0.00	-0.11	-0.13	-0.15	-0.01	0.01	-0.08
Proportion African-American	-0.34	0.06	-0.11	-0.07	0.09	-0.24	0.11	-0.13
Different MSA 5 years ago	-0.06	0.06	-0.02	0.20	0.37	-0.18	-0.01	-0.17
% Jobs/% residents in central city	-0.04	-0.02	0.09	0.00	0.05	0.10	0.02	0.07
Hholds headed by over age 65	-0.13	-0.01	-0.10	-0.31	-0.29	0.29	0.43	-0.18
Hholds headed by woman	-0.10	0.12	0.00	-0.39	-0.31	0.23	0.42	-0.03
Households with no earner	-0.07	0.04	-0.17	-0.51	-0.62	0.42	0.54	-0.23
Hholds with multi earners	-0.01	0.10	0.11	0.74	0.54	-0.38	-0.36	-0.08
Hhold size	1.00	0.11	0.08	-0.12	-0.03	0.09	-0.52	0.39
Gini coeff on ed	0.11	1.00	-0.14	0.14	-0.11	0.04	0.11	-0.40
Median ed, 25–64 yrs. old	0.08	-0.14	1.00	0.04	0.25	0.04	-0.08	0.10
Employ/pop, 25–64 yr. olds	-0.12	0.14	0.04	1.00	0.36	-0.32	-0.32	-0.24
Per capita income	-0.03	-0.11	0.25	0.36	1.00	-0.34	-0.27	0.06
Gini coeff on earnings	0.09	0.04	0.04	-0.32	-0.34	1.00	0.48	0.06
Gini coeff on hhold income	-0.52	0.11	-0.08	-0.32	-0.27	0.48	1.00	-0.47
1980 Gini coeff hhold income	0.39	-0.40	0.10	-0.24	0.06	0.06	-0.47	1.00
Residential segregation index	-0.05	0.01	-0.24	0.04	-0.01	0.01	0.12	-0.18

Table A.2 Statistics on Income Distribution in 1979 and 1989, by MSA

	Gini coefficient on earnings for all workers	1979 Gini coefficient on earnings for all workers	Gini coefficient on household income	1979 Gini coefficient on household income	Quintile 1	Quintile 2	Quintile 3	Quintile 4	Quintile 5
Birmingham, AL	0.015	0.458	0.066	0.415	-0.0056	-0.0094	-0.0104	-0.0095	0.0348
Mobile, AL	0.070	0.459	0.096	0.417	-0.0084	-0.0199	-0.0162	-0.0088	0.0532
Montgomery, AL	0.044	0.447	0.076	0.413	-0.0020	-0.0094	-0.0124	-0.0094	0.0331
Little Rock, AR	0.074	0.432	0.092	0.389	-0.0072	-0.0152	-0.0110	-0.0095	0.0429
Phoenix, AZ	0.037	0.458	0.078	0.384	-0.0070	-0.0238	-0.0139	-0.0043	0.0491
Tucson, AZ	0.040	0.474	0.082	0.398	-0.0036	-0.0129	-0.0115	-0.0093	0.0373
Anaheim/Santa Anna, CA	0.039	0.457	0.145	0.341	-0.0030	-0.0058	-0.0106	-0.0119	0.0313
Bakersfield, CA	0.020	0.464	0.125	0.372	0.0018	-0.0017	-0.0068	-0.0105	0.0171
Chico, CA	0.024	0.509	0.075	0.406	0.0034	0.0017	-0.0025	-0.0111	0.0085
Fresno, CA	0.048	0.474	0.126	0.387	0.0029	-0.0022	-0.0091	-0.0149	0.0233
Los Angeles/Long Beach, CA	0.065	0.453	0.070	0.414	-0.0040	-0.0071	-0.0096	-0.0123	0.0330
Modesto, CA	0.010	0.468	0.108	0.375	0.0016	-0.0027	-0.0067	-0.0107	0.0186
Oxnard/Simi Valley/Ventura, CA	0.012	0.465	0.097	0.344	0.0036	0.0007	-0.0035	-0.0083	0.0075
Riverside/San Ber./Ont., CA	0.026	0.444	0.116	0.362	0.0003	-0.0240	-0.0129	-0.0058	0.0424
Sacramento, CA	-0.007	0.454	0.082	0.370	-0.0008	-0.0003	-0.0038	-0.0095	0.0145

Salinas/Seaside/Monterey, CA	0.003	0.457	0.062	0.368	0.0007	0.0172	-0.0006	-0.0134	-0.0039
San Diego, CA	0.007	0.466	0.024	0.397	0.0027	0.0070	-0.0001	-0.0112	0.0015
San Francisco/Oakland, CA	0.063	0.444	0.117	0.373	-0.0037	-0.0058	-0.0140	-0.0170	0.0404
San Jose, CA	0.013	0.447	0.135	0.334	-0.0029	-0.0049	-0.0098	-0.0092	0.0267
Santa Barbara/S. Maria/Lompoc, CA	0.039	0.489	0.144	0.372	-0.0037	-0.0100	-0.0057	-0.0096	0.0289
Santa Cruz, CA	0.020	0.495	0.041	0.391	0.0010	0.0031	0.0039	-0.0021	-0.0059
Santa Rosa, CA	-0.013	0.462	0.001	0.389	0.0042	0.0068	0.0006	-0.0124	0.0009
Stockton, CA	-0.043	0.453	-0.024	0.382	0.0092	0.0089	0.0005	-0.0097	-0.0089
Vallejo/Fairfield/Napa, CA	-0.038	0.451	0.069	0.349	0.0051	0.0077	-0.0021	-0.0100	-0.0007
Visalia/Tulare/Porterville, CA	0.051	0.468	0.123	0.388	0.0057	-0.0033	-0.0086	-0.0076	0.0138
Colorado Springs, CO	0.007	0.461	0.081	0.363	-0.0002	-0.0117	-0.0043	-0.0031	0.0192
Denver, CO	0.044	0.455	0.125	0.352	-0.0041	-0.0079	-0.0093	-0.0071	0.0283
Fort Collins/Loveland, CO	0.018	0.494	0.115	0.356	0.0025	0.0150	-0.0035	-0.0083	-0.0057
Bridgeport/Milford, CT	-0.089	0.469	0.085	0.382	-0.0003	0.0008	-0.0029	-0.0020	0.0045
Hartford, CT	0.029	0.447	0.186	0.355	-0.0029	-0.0078	-0.0141	-0.0135	0.0383
New Haven/Meriden, CT	-0.085	0.474	0.071	0.388	-0.0020	-0.0135	-0.0006	0.0043	0.0119
Stamford, CT	0.039	0.469	0.186	0.371	-0.0071	-0.0107	-0.0168	-0.0156	0.0502

(continued)

Table A.2 (continued)

	Gini coefficient on earnings for all workers	1979 Gini coefficient on earnings for all workers	Gini coefficient on household income	1979 Gini coefficient on household income	Quintile 1	Quintile 2	Quintile 3	Quintile 4	Quintile 5
Waterbury, CT	-0.056	0.404	-0.009	0.387	-0.0057	-0.0004	0.0104	0.0073	-0.0116
Washington, DC	-0.015	0.445	0.035	0.367	-0.0011	-0.0004	-0.0033	-0.0125	0.0173
Wilmington, DE	-0.029	0.472	0.011	0.383	0.0045	0.0090	-0.0034	-0.0117	0.0015
Bradenton, FL	0.011	0.455	0.034	0.386	0.0001	0.0054	0.0004	-0.0021	-0.0038
Daytona Beach, FL	-0.003	0.474	0.039	0.400	0.0001	-0.0239	-0.0015	0.0060	0.0194
Ft. Lauderdale, FL	0.018	0.455	0.131	0.379	-0.0039	-0.0265	-0.0137	-0.0018	0.0458
Fort Myers/Cape Corral, FL	0.047	0.449	0.067	0.380	0.0003	-0.0111	-0.0072	-0.0066	0.0245
Gainesville, FL	0.010	0.518	0.111	0.425	-0.0002	-0.0161	-0.0122	-0.0133	0.0418
Jacksonville, FL	0.016	0.442	0.069	0.388	-0.0053	-0.0104	-0.0048	-0.0092	0.0296
Lakeland/Winter Haven, FL	0.017	0.455	0.040	0.379	0.0001	0.0014	-0.0047	-0.0139	0.0172
Melbourne/Titusville/Palm Bay, FL	0.008	0.459	0.098	0.359	-0.0055	-0.0097	-0.0066	-0.0063	0.0281
Miami, FL	0.032	0.463	0.134	0.417	-0.0052	-0.0129	-0.0130	-0.0104	0.0414
Orlando, FL	0.014	0.457	0.079	0.378	-0.0056	-0.0088	-0.0041	-0.0054	0.0238
Pensacola, FL	0.049	0.452	0.115	0.384	-0.0031	-0.0178	-0.0106	-0.0118	0.0434
Sarasota, FL	0.030	0.475	0.096	0.382	0.0002	-0.0075	-0.0076	-0.0085	0.0234

Tampa/St. Petersburg, Fl	0.010	0.489	0.089	0.406	-0.0022	-0.0180	-0.0064	-0.0036	0.0301
West Palm/Boca Raton, Fl	0.035	0.459	0.119	0.386	0.0003	-0.0149	-0.0119	-0.0107	0.0372
Atlanta, GA	0.029	0.471	0.099	0.391	-0.0068	-0.0085	-0.0091	-0.0099	0.0344
Augusta, GA	0.068	0.456	0.038	0.414	0.0004	0.0203	0.0089	-0.0037	-0.0259
Macon/Warner Robbins, GA	0.077	0.450	0.183	0.374	-0.0062	-0.0184	-0.0199	-0.0159	0.0604
Savannah, GA	0.035	0.447	0.085	0.399	-0.0064	-0.0138	-0.0061	-0.0061	0.0324
Cedar Rapids, IA	0.061	0.436	0.159	0.407	0.0027	-0.0034	-0.0104	-0.0074	0.0185
Des Moines, IA	0.044	0.432	0.100	0.325	0.0000	-0.0044	-0.0133	-0.0159	0.0335
Boise City, ID	0.023	0.443	0.056	0.368	0.0030	-0.0006	-0.0062	-0.0135	0.0172
Champaign/Urbana/ Rantoul, IL	-0.025	0.466	0.069	0.380	0.0002	0.0420	0.0184	-0.0103	-0.0503
Chicago, IL	0.059	0.510	0.088	0.381	-0.0018	-0.0052	-0.0132	-0.0153	0.0355
Davenport/Rock Island/ Moline, IL	0.049	0.426	0.101	0.350	-0.0060	-0.0142	-0.0181	-0.0022	0.0406
Peoria, IL	0.056	0.436	0.151	0.386	0.0035	-0.0062	-0.0106	-0.0019	0.0152
Rockford, IL	0.037	0.451	0.157	0.346	-0.0019	-0.0065	-0.0135	-0.0081	0.0300
Springfield, IL	0.022	0.434	0.138	0.335	0.0027	-0.0009	-0.0096	-0.0129	0.0207
Ft. Wayne, IN	0.040	0.443	0.158	0.360	-0.0035	-0.0073	-0.0104	-0.0095	0.0307
Gary/Hammond, IN	0.070	0.439	0.177	0.332	-0.0040	-0.0120	-0.0178	-0.0038	0.0376
Indianapolis, IN	0.041	0.434	0.155	0.339	-0.0005	-0.0056	-0.0122	-0.0130	0.0312

(continued)

Table A.2 (continued)

	Gini coefficient on earnings for all workers	1979 Gini coefficient on earnings for all workers	Gini coefficient on household income	1979 Gini coefficient on household income	Quintile 1	Quintile 2	Quintile 3	Quintile 4	Quintile 5
South Bend, IN	0.041	0.443	0.163	0.350	-0.0003	-0.0045	-0.0113	-0.0122	0.0283
Wichita, KS	0.042	0.458	0.070	0.347	-0.0054	-0.0106	-0.0098	-0.0048	0.0306
Lexington, KY	0.029	0.427	0.054	0.376	0.0005	-0.0040	-0.0026	-0.0089	0.0151
Louisville, KY	0.095	0.482	0.093	0.412	-0.0015	-0.0059	-0.0152	-0.0143	0.0368
Alexandria, LA	0.000	0.441	0.098	0.397	-0.0002	-0.0074	-0.0098	-0.0087	0.0262
Baton Rouge, LA	0.049	0.463	0.154	0.415	-0.0024	-0.0131	-0.0158	-0.0119	0.0431
Lafayette, LA	0.026	0.470	0.186	0.386	-0.0078	-0.0249	-0.0215	-0.0019	0.0561
New Orleans, LA	0.051	0.484	0.162	0.388	-0.0067	-0.0293	-0.0237	-0.0139	0.0736
Shreveport, LA	0.047	0.461	0.143	0.412	-0.0083	-0.0233	-0.0180	-0.0037	0.0532
Boston, MA	0.019	0.448	0.126	0.399	-0.0013	-0.0030	-0.0049	-0.0088	0.0179
Fall River, MA	0.006	0.435	0.072	0.294	-0.0068	-0.0149	-0.0045	0.0014	0.0248
Lawrence, MA	-0.007	0.453	0.063	0.400	-0.0117	-0.0208	-0.0150	0.0057	0.0418
Lowell, MA	-0.023	0.400	0.279	0.400	-0.0135	-0.0414	-0.0160	0.0093	0.0616
Worcester, MA	-0.011	0.453	0.034	0.374	0.0001	-0.0087	-0.0005	0.0018	0.0073
Baltimore, MD	0.009	0.398	0.054	0.391	-0.0006	-0.0004	-0.0070	-0.0128	0.0208
Ann Arbor, MI	0.025	0.439	0.147	0.383	0.0002	0.0063	-0.0058	-0.0150	0.0143
Benton Harbor, MI	0.006	0.494	0.103	0.356	0.0000	0.0013	-0.0017	-0.0114	0.0118
Detroit, MI	0.067	0.462	0.097	0.362	-0.0033	-0.0086	-0.0132	-0.0101	0.0351

Flint, MI	0.094	0.443	0.193	0.382	-0.0057	-0.0133	-0.0139	-0.0038	0.0366
Grand Rapids, MI	0.028	0.425	0.115	0.343	0.0026	0.0021	-0.0064	-0.0081	0.0099
Jackson, MI	-0.002	0.454	0.135	0.341	0.0107	0.0193	-0.0010	-0.0146	-0.0144
Kalamazoo, MI	0.044	0.455	0.152	0.344	0.0047	0.0015	-0.0086	-0.0132	0.0156
Lansing, MI	0.008	0.471	0.043	0.351	0.0063	0.0083	-0.0036	-0.0086	-0.0023
Saginaw, MI	0.086	0.472	0.191	0.366	-0.0002	-0.0124	-0.0158	-0.0034	0.0317
Duluth, MN	0.007	0.502	0.058	0.388	0.0001	-0.0408	-0.0317	-0.0044	0.0767
Minneapolis, MN	0.010	0.456	0.070	0.375	0.0023	-0.0005	-0.0105	-0.0146	0.0232
St. Cloud, MN	-0.068	0.441	-0.000	0.344	0.0030	0.0449	0.0172	-0.0203	-0.0448
Kansas City, MO	0.035	0.450	0.074	0.384	-0.0036	-0.0061	-0.0119	-0.0153	0.0369
Springfield, MO	0.036	0.453	0.077	0.365	0.0043	0.0030	-0.0046	-0.0256	0.0228
St. Louis, MO	0.045	0.482	0.080	0.404	-0.0042	-0.0091	-0.0123	-0.0104	0.0360
Biloxi/Gulfport, MS	0.032	0.443	0.109	0.378	-0.0000	-0.0186	-0.0117	-0.0043	0.0346
Jackson, MS	0.061	0.461	0.100	0.391	-0.0056	-0.0243	-0.0162	-0.0105	0.0565
Charlotte/Gastonia, NC	0.003	0.462	0.134	0.424	-0.0045	-0.0108	-0.0090	-0.0045	0.0288
Fayetteville, NC	0.017	0.443	0.055	0.360	0.0003	0.0226	0.0050	-0.0085	-0.0193
Greensboro/Winston/High Pt., NC	0.022	0.417	0.141	0.378	0.0014	-0.0031	-0.0078	-0.0147	0.0242
Raleigh/Durham, NC	-0.009	0.448	0.100	0.369	0.0044	0.0081	-0.0012	-0.0133	0.0020
Lincon, NE	-0.004	0.461	0.033	0.358	0.0062	0.0111	0.0006	-0.0113	-0.0066
Omaha, NE	0.018	0.470	0.039	0.376	0.0014	0.0006	-0.0064	-0.0123	0.0167

(continued)

Table A.2 (continued)

	Gini coefficient on earnings for all workers	1979 Gini coefficient on earnings for all workers	Gini coefficient on household income	1979 Gini coefficient on household income	Quintile 1	Quintile 2	Quintile 3	Quintile 4	Quintile 5
Atlantic City, NJ	-0.067	0.456	0.065	0.386	0.0004	-0.0128	0.0027	-0.0024	0.0121
Jersey City, NJ	0.036	0.458	0.092	0.377	-0.0096	-0.0124	-0.0065	-0.0052	0.0336
Newark, NJ	0.040	0.400	0.163	0.396	-0.0049	-0.0085	-0.0132	-0.0155	0.0421
Trenton, NJ	0.008	0.456	0.127	0.372	0.0033	0.0042	-0.0061	-0.0136	0.0123
Albuquerque, NM	0.036	0.456	0.070	0.358	-0.0048	-0.0114	-0.0104	-0.0062	0.0328
Las Vegas, NV	0.028	0.466	0.058	0.394	-0.0060	-0.0099	-0.0081	-0.0081	0.0321
Reno, NV	0.026	0.437	0.118	0.386	-0.0027	-0.0142	-0.0102	-0.0107	0.0378
Albany/Schnec./Troy, NY	0.004	0.432	0.122	0.375	-0.0029	-0.0056	-0.0070	-0.0087	0.0241
Buffalo, NY	0.042	0.452	0.169	0.350	-0.0047	-0.0088	-0.0132	-0.0085	0.0353
Nassau/Suffolk, NY	0.029	0.448	0.124	0.356	-0.0038	-0.0113	-0.0151	-0.0121	0.0424
New York (incl. N.Y. suburbs), NY	0.061	0.441	0.091	0.353	-0.0066	-0.0120	-0.0099	-0.0109	0.0394
Rochester, NY	0.007	0.464	0.129	0.350	-0.0044	-0.0070	-0.0077	-0.0073	0.0265
Syracuse, NY	0.003	0.457	0.151	0.348	0.0011	-0.0034	-0.0081	-0.0087	0.0192
Utica/Rome, NY	0.011	0.459	0.133	0.346	-0.0025	-0.0111	-0.0112	-0.0042	0.0290
Akron, OH	0.056	0.436	0.191	0.439	-0.0042	-0.0114	-0.0155	-0.0096	0.0406
Canton, OH	0.071	0.457	0.183	0.348	0.0030	-0.0032	-0.0153	-0.0174	0.0330
Cleveland, OH	0.066	0.431	0.173	0.338	-0.0030	-0.0084	-0.0142	-0.0128	0.0383

Cincinnati, OH	0.053	0.431	0.098	0.377	0.0001	-0.0055	-0.0124	-0.0163	0.0340
Columbus, OH	0.038	0.438	0.078	0.362	0.0028	-0.0001	-0.0089	-0.0159	0.0221
Dayton/Springfield, OH	0.035	0.450	0.079	0.380	0.0004	-0.0057	-0.0118	-0.0095	0.0267
Hamilton, OH	0.026	0.449	0.132	0.375	0.0011	-0.0010	-0.0103	-0.0073	0.0175
Lima, OH	0.083	0.462	0.088	0.342	-0.0091	-0.0179	-0.0144	-0.0033	0.0447
Lorain/Elyria, OH	0.069	0.434	0.167	0.363	0.0027	-0.0045	-0.0137	-0.0073	0.0228
Toledo, OH	0.072	0.451	0.116	0.389	-0.0007	-0.0063	-0.0139	-0.0123	0.0332
Youngstown/Warren, OH	0.091	0.428	0.096	0.324	-0.0054	-0.0103	-0.0171	-0.0077	0.0405
Oklahoma City, OK	0.040	0.455	0.071	0.381	-0.0066	-0.0214	-0.0125	-0.0053	0.0457
Tulsa, OK	0.064	0.453	0.112	0.394	-0.0080	-0.0185	-0.0188	-0.0114	0.0567
Eugene/Springfield, OR	0.017	0.455	0.117	0.396	0.0014	-0.0005	-0.0095	-0.0107	0.0192
Portland, OR	0.027	0.470	0.071	0.386	0.0003	-0.0007	-0.0096	-0.0140	0.0240
Salem, OR	-0.007	0.487	0.018	0.371	0.0087	0.0101	0.0016	-0.0111	-0.0094
Allentown, PA	0.015	0.450	0.130	0.381	-0.0005	-0.0014	-0.0089	-0.0094	0.0201
Erie, PA	0.066	0.439	0.164	0.338	-0.0004	-0.0054	-0.0131	-0.0110	0.0299
Harrisburg/Lebanon/Carlyle, PA	0.003	0.445	0.099	0.343	0.0031	0.0015	-0.0047	-0.0085	0.0086
Johnstown, PA	0.006	0.423	0.145	0.341	-0.0065	-0.0079	-0.0108	-0.0068	0.0319
Lancaster, PA	0.023	0.449	0.096	0.353	0.0036	0.0021	-0.0058	-0.0094	0.0096
Philadelphia, PA	0.028	0.414	0.042	0.327	0.0018	0.0056	-0.0028	-0.0130	0.0084

(continued)

Table A.2 (continued)

	Gini coefficient on earnings for all workers	1979 Gini coefficient on earnings for all workers	Gini coefficient on household income	1979 Gini coefficient on household income	Quintile 1	Quintile 2	Quintile 3	Quintile 4	Quintile 5
Pittsburgh, PA	0.101	0.433	0.237	0.332	-0.0043	-0.0137	-0.0227	-0.0167	0.0573
Reading, PA	-0.015	0.440	0.087	0.354	-0.0008	0.0007	-0.0026	-0.0049	0.0077
York, PA	0.001	0.431	0.101	0.341	0.0052	0.0034	-0.0056	-0.0052	0.0021
Providence, RI	0.050	0.448	0.085	0.394	-0.0079	-0.0312	-0.0206	-0.0018	0.0615
Charleston, SC	0.033	0.448	0.109	0.412	0.0001	-0.0203	-0.0122	-0.0035	0.0359
Columbia, SC	0.006	0.451	0.088	0.370	0.0000	0.0160	0.0033	-0.0108	-0.0084
Greenville, SC	0.050	0.435	0.131	0.371	-0.0004	-0.0078	-0.0100	-0.0083	0.0265
Chattanooga, TN	0.052	0.443	0.098	0.400	-0.0013	-0.0066	-0.0124	-0.0169	0.0372
Johnson City/Kingsport/Bristol, TN	0.061	0.444	0.070	0.399	-0.0120	-0.0188	-0.0157	0.0022	0.0444
Knoxville, TN	0.024	0.470	0.121	0.391	-0.0023	-0.0069	-0.0114	-0.0111	0.0316
Memphis, TN	0.059	0.462	0.088	0.425	-0.0041	-0.0117	-0.0137	-0.0163	0.0457
Nashville, TN	0.006	0.454	0.061	0.394	-0.0046	-0.0100	-0.0080	-0.0082	0.0307
Austin, TX	0.012	0.472	0.118	0.388	0.0002	0.0029	-0.0053	-0.0145	0.0167
Beaumont/Port Arthur/Orange, TX	0.066	0.446	0.187	0.361	-0.0067	-0.0187	-0.0233	-0.0031	0.0517
Brownsville/Harlingen, TX	0.070	0.468	0.117	0.426	-0.0025	-0.0456	-0.0264	-0.0087	0.0832

Corpus Christi, TX	0.039	0.464	0.170	0.381	-0.0083	-0.0369	-0.0243	-0.0010	0.0705
Dallas/Ft. Worth, TX	0.055	0.449	0.059	0.386	-0.0068	-0.0152	-0.0142	-0.0103	0.0464
El Paso, TX	0.068	0.454	0.122	0.395	0.0003	-0.0097	-0.0089	-0.0087	0.0269
Houston, TX	0.089	0.443	0.156	0.377	-0.0029	-0.0186	-0.0222	-0.0148	0.0585
Killeen/Temple, TX	0.016	0.429	0.076	0.380	0.0003	0.0388	0.0140	-0.0101	-0.0429
Longview/Marshall, TX	0.026	0.461	0.146	0.374	-0.0033	-0.0094	-0.0139	-0.0066	0.0333
Lubbock, TX	0.053	0.474	0.169	0.384	0.0009	-0.0035	-0.0106	-0.0117	0.0249
McAllen/Edinburg/Mission, TX	0.060	0.490	0.143	0.427	-0.0007	-0.0327	-0.0258	-0.0122	0.0712
San Antonio, TX	0.064	0.456	0.134	0.394	-0.0021	-0.0132	-0.0136	-0.0113	0.0402
Waco, TX	-0.003	0.476	0.095	0.401	-0.0020	-0.0185	-0.0061	0.0036	0.0230
Provo/Orem, UT	0.003	0.535	0.101	0.351	0.0040	0.0010	-0.0011	-0.0042	0.0005
Salt Lake City/Ogden, UT	0.032	0.462	0.070	0.363	-0.0032	-0.0071	-0.0091	-0.0076	0.0269
Norfolk/Va. Beach/Newport News, VA	-0.009	0.442	-0.011	0.393	-0.0000	0.0074	0.0039	-0.0079	-0.0035
Richmond, VA	0.023	0.437	0.119	0.356	0.0028	0.0012	-0.0081	-0.0108	0.0149
Roanoke, VA	0.008	0.441	0.068	0.389	-0.0033	-0.0081	-0.0124	-0.0067	0.0304
Bremerton, WA	0.022	0.435	0.096	0.341	0.0041	0.0097	-0.0053	-0.0131	0.0046
Richland/Kennewick/Pasco, WA	0.066	0.440	0.234	0.319	-0.0004	-0.0174	-0.0248	-0.0066	0.0492

(continued)

Table A.2 (continued)

	Gini coefficient on earnings for all workers	1979 Gini coefficient on earnings for all workers	Gini coefficient on household income	1979 Gini coefficient on household income	Quintile 1	Quintile 2	Quintile 3	Quintile 4	Quintile 5
Seattle/Everett, WA	0.011	0.445	0.128	0.346	0.0040	0.0033	-0.0099	-0.0147	0.0174
Spokane, WA	0.018	0.465	0.136	0.363	0.0042	0.0004	-0.0091	-0.0114	0.0159
Tacoma, WA	-0.015	0.453	0.066	0.363	0.0068	0.0127	0.0019	-0.0151	-0.0063
Yakima, WA	0.029	0.476	0.129	0.380	-0.0008	-0.0039	-0.0088	-0.0121	0.0255
Appleton/Oshkosh/Neenah, WI	-0.009	0.458	0.117	0.326	0.0038	0.0027	-0.0070	-0.0100	0.0105
Green Bay, WI	0.041	0.450	0.149	0.330	0.0048	0.0005	-0.0098	-0.0107	0.0153
Janesville/Beloit, WI	0.039	0.434	0.105	0.331	0.0066	0.0080	-0.0075	-0.0089	0.0018
Madison, WI	-0.033	0.475	0.064	0.350	0.0116	0.0178	0.0019	-0.0182	-0.0130
Milwaukee, WI	0.049	0.442	0.166	0.342	-0.0011	-0.0063	-0.0113	-0.0097	0.0284
Racine, WI	0.079	0.435	0.174	0.322	0.0014	-0.0027	-0.0117	-0.0131	0.0261
Huntington/Ashland, WV	0.039	0.458	0.112	0.414	-0.0042	-0.0149	-0.0149	-0.0075	0.0417

References

Abramson, Alan J., Mitchell S. Tobin, and Matthew S. VanderGoot. 1995. "The Changing Geography of Metropolitan Opportunity: The Segregation of the Poor in U.S. Metropolitan Areas, 1970–1990." *Housing Policy Debate* 6(1): 45–72.

Barro, Robert J., and Xavier Sala-i-Martin. 1992. "Convergence." *Journal of Political Economy* 100(2): 223–251.

Bartik, Timothy. 1991. *Who Benefits From State and Local Economic Development Policies?* Kalamazoo, Michigan: W.E. Upjohn Institute for Employment Research.

Benabou, Roland. 1996. "Inequality and Growth." In *NBER Macroeconomics Annual 1996*, Ben S. Bernanke and Julio J. Rotenberg, eds., Cambridge, Massachusetts: MIT Press.

_____. 1993. "Workings of a City: Locations, Education, and Production." *Quarterly Journal of Economics* 108(3): 619–652.

Blackburn, McKinley L., David E. Bloom, and Richard B. Freeman. 1990. "An Era of Falling Earnings and Rising Inequality?" *The Brookings Review* (Winter): 38–43.

Blackburn, McKinley L., and David Bloom. 1987. "Earnings and Income Inequality in the United States." *Population and Development Review* 13(4): 575–609.

Blank, Rebecca, and David Card. 1993. "Poverty, Income-Distribution, and Growth, Are they Still Connected?" *Brookings Papers on Economic Activity* 0(2): 285–339.

Blinder, Alan S. 1974. *Toward an Economic Theory of Income Distribution.* Cambridge, Massachusetts: MIT Press.

Bluestone, Barry, and Bennett Harrison. 1986. *The Great American Job Machine: The Proliferation of Low-Wage Employment in the U.S. Economy.* Study prepared for the Joint Economic Committee. Washington, D.C.: Government Printing Office, December.

Bobo, Lawrence. 1991. "Social Responsibility, Individualism and Redistributive Policies." *Sociological Forum* 6(1): 71–92.

Borjas, George. 1995. "Ethnicity, Neighborhoods, and Human Capital Externalities." *American Economic Review* 85(3): 365–389.

Boskin, Michael J., and Dale W. Jorgenson. 1997. "Implications of Overstating Inflation for Indexing Government Programs and Understanding Economic Progress." *American Economic Review* 87(2): 89–93.

Bound, John, and George Johnson. 1992. "Changes in the Structure of Wages During the 1980s: An Evaluation of Alternative Explanations." *American Economic Review* 82(3): 371–92.

_____. 1991. "Wages in the United States During the 1980s and Beyond." In *Workers and Their Wages: Changing Patterns in the United States*, Marvin Kosters, ed. Washington, D.C.: AEI Press.

Browne, Lynn E. 1989. "Shifting Regional Fortunes: The Wheel Turns." *New England Economic Review* (May/June): 27–40.

Burtless, Gary. A. 1990. *Future of Lousy Jobs? The Changing Structure of U.S. Wages*. Washington, D.C.: The Brookings Institution.

Carlino, Gerald A. 1986. "Do Regional Wages Differ?" *Business Review* (July/August): 17–25.

Case, Anne, and Lawrence Katz. 1991. "The Company You Keep: The Effects of Family and Neighborhood on Disadvantages Youths." National Bureau of Economic Research working paper no. 3705, Cambridge, Massashusetts.

Card, David. 1989. "Deregulation and Labor Earnings in the Airline Industry." Working paper no. 247, Industrial Relations Section, Princeton University, January.

_____. 1996. "The Effect of Unions on the Structure of Wages: A Longitudinal Analysis." *Econometrica* 64(4): 957–979.

Cloutier, Norman R. 1997. "Metropolitan Income Inequality During the 1980s: The Impact of Urban Development, Industrial Mix and Family Structure." *Journal of Regional Science* 37(3): 459–478.

Crane, Jonathan. 1991. "The Epidemic Theory of Ghettos and Neighborhood Effects on Dropping Out and Teenage Childbearing." *American Journal of Sociology* 96(5): 1226–1259.

Cutler, David M., and Edward L. Glaeser. 1997. "Are Ghettos Good or Bad?" *Quarterly Journal of Economics* 112(3): 827–872.

Cutler, David M., and Lawrence F. Katz. 1992. "Rising Inequality? Changes in the Distribution of Income and Consumption in the 1980's." *American Economic Review* 82(2): 546–51.

Danziger, Sheldon. 1976. "Determinants of the Level and Distribution of Family Income in Metropolitan Areas, 1969." *Land Economics* 52(4): 467–478.

Dickie, Mark, and Shelby Gerking. 1988. "Interregional Wage Differentials in the United States: A Survey." In *Migration and Labor Market Adjustment*, Alan Schlottmann, et al., eds. Boston: Kluwer Academic Publishers.

Eberts, Randall W. 1989. "Accounting for the Recent Divergence In Regional Wage Differentials." *Economic Review* (Third Quarter): 14–26.

Farber, Stephen C., and Robert J. Newman. 1987. "Accounting for South/Non-South Real Wage Differentials and for Changes in Those Differentials Over Time." *Review of Economics and Statistics* 69(2): 215–23.

Farbman, Michael. 1975. "The Size Distribution of Family Income in U.S. SMSAs, 1959." *Review of Income and Wealth* 21(2): 217–237.

Farley, Reynolds, and William H. Frey. 1993. "Changes in the Segregation of Whites from Blacks During the 1980s: Small Steps toward a More Racially Integrated Society." *American Sociological Review* (February): 23–45.

Freeman, Richard. 1992. "How Much Has De-Unionization Contributed to the Rise in Male Earnings Inequality?" In *Uneven Tides: Rising Inequality in America*, Sheldon Danziger and Peter Gottschalk, eds. New York: Sage Press.

Freeman, Richard. 1996. "Labor Market Institutions and Earnings Inequality." *New England Economic Review* (May/June): 157–168.

Galster, George, G. McCorkhill, and S. Gopalan. 1988. "The Determinants of Income Inequality in Metropolitan Areas." *Review of Business* 10(2): 17–22.

Garofalo, Gasper, and Michael S. Fogarty. 1979. "Urban Inequality and City Size: An Examination of Alternative Hypotheses for Large and Small Cities." *Review of Economics and Statistics* 61(3): 381–388.

Gerking, Shelby, and William Weirick. 1983. "Compensating Differences and Interregional Wage Differentials." *Review of Economics and Statistics* (August): 483–87.

Getis, Arthur. 1988. "Economic Heterogeneity within Large Metropolitan Areas." *Growth and Change* (Winter): 31–42.

Gottschalk, Peter, and Sheldon Danziger. 1993. *Uneven Tides: Rising Inequality in America*. New York: Russell Sage Foundation.

Haworth, Charles, J. Long, and David Rasmussen. 1978. "Income Distribution, City Size, and Urban Growth." *Urban Studies* 15: 1–7.

_____. 1982. "Income Distribution, City Size, and Urban Growth: The Final Reply." *Urban Studies* 19(1): 75–77.

Henle, Peter. 1972. "Exploring the Distribution of Earned Income." *Monthly Labor Review* 95(12): 16–27.

Henle, Peter, and Ryscavage, Paul. 1980. "The Distribution of Earned Income Among Men and Women, 1958–1977." *Monthly Labor Review* 103(4): 3–10.

Holzer, Harry J. 1991. "The Spatial Mismatch Hypothesis: What Has the Evidence Shown?" *Urban Studies* 28(1): 105–22.

Ihlanfeldt, Keith R. 1992. *Job Accessibility and the Employment and School Enrollment of Teenagers*. Kalamazoo, Michigan: W.E. Upjohn Institute for Employment Research.

Jencks, Christopher, and Susan E. Mayer. 1990. "Residential Segregation, Job Proximity, and Black Job Opportunities." In *Inner-City Poverty in the United States*, Lawrence E. Lynn, Jr., and Michael G.H. McGearyk, eds. Washington, D.C.: National Academy Press.

Juhn, Chinhui. 1999. "Wage Inequality and Demand for Skill: Evidence from Five Decades." *Industrial and Labor Relations Review* 52(3): 424–443.

Juhn, Chinhui, and Kevin Murphy. 1992. "Wage Inequality and Family Labor Supply." Paper presented at the American Economic Association meetings in New Orleans, January.

Juhn, Chinhui, Kevin Murphy, and Brooks Pierce. 1994. "Wage Inequality and the Rise in the Returns to Skill." *Journal of Political Economy* 101(3): 410–442.

Kain, John F. 1968. "Housing Segregation, Negro Employment, and Metropolitan Decentralization." *Quarterly Journal of Economics* (May): 175–197.

_____. 1992. "The Spatial Mismatch Hypothesis: Three Decades Later." Housing Policy Debate 3(2): 371–460.

Karoly, Lynn. 1988. A Study of the Distribution of Individual Earnings in the United States from 1967 to 1986. Ph.D. dissertation at Yale University.

Karoly, Lynn A. 1992. "Changes in the Distribution of Individual Earnings in the United States: 1967–1986." *Review of Economics and Statistics* 74(1): 107–15.

Karoly, Lynn A., and Jacob Alex Klerman. 1992. "Regional Differences in Earning Inequality." Paper presented to the American Economic Association meetings in New Orleans, January.

Karoly, Lynn A., and Gary Burtless. 1995. "Demographic Change, Rising Earnings Inequality, and the Distribution of Personal Well-Being, 1959–1989." *Demography* 32(3): 379–405.

Kasarda, John D. 1993. "Inner-City Concentrated Poverty and Neighborhood Distress: 1970–1990." *Housing Policy Debate* 4(3): 253–302.

Katz, Lawrence F., and Kevin M. Murphy. 1992. "Changes in Relative Wages, 1963–1987: Supply and Demand Factors." *Quarterly Journal of Economics* 107(1): 35–78.

Katz, Lawrence F., and Ana L. Revenga. 1989. "Changes in the Structure of Wages: The U.S. vs. Japan." *Journal of the Japanese and International Economies* 3(4): 522–53.

Kosters, Marvin H., and Murray N. Ross. 1987. "The Distribution of Earnings and Employment Opportunities: A Re-Examination of the Evidence." American Enterprise Occasional Papers, September.

Kosters, Marvin H. 1988. "The Quality of Jobs: Evidence from the Distribution of Annual Earnings and Hourly Wages." American Enterprise Occasional Papers, July.

Levy, Frank. 1989. "Recent Trends in U.S. Earnings and Family Incomes." *NBER Annual*. Cambridge: MIT Press, pp. 73–113.

Levy, Frank, and Richard J. Murnane. 1992. "U.S. Earnings Level and Earning Inequality: A Review of Recent Trends and Proposed Explanations." *Journal of Economic Literature* 30(3): 1333–81.

J. Long, D. Rasmussen, and C. Haworth. 1977. "Income Inequality and City Size." *Review of Economics and Statistics* 59(2): 244–246.

Madden, Janice F., and William Stull. 1991. *Work, Wages, and Poverty: Income Distribution in Post-Industrial Philadelphia*. Philadelphia: University of Pennsylvania Press.

Manski, Charles F. 1993. "Identification of Endogenous Social Effects: The Reflection Problem." *Review of Economic Studies* 60(3): 531–542.

Massey, Douglas. 1999. "The Residential Segregation of Blacks, Hispanics, and Asians: 1970 to 1990." In *Immigration and Race Relations*, Gerald D. Haynes, ed. New Haven: Yale University Press.

Massey, Douglas, and Nancy Denton. 1993. *American Apartheid: Segregation and the Making of the Underclass*. Cambridge, MA: Harvard University Press.

Mayer, Christopher J. 1996. "Does Location Matter?" *New England Economic Review* (May/June): 26–40.

Michel, Richard C. 1991. "Economic Growth and Income Equality Since the 1982 Recession." *Journal of Policy Analysis and Management* 2(10): 181–203.

Moffitt, Robert A. 1990. "The Distribution of Earnings and the Welfare State." In *A Future of Lousy Jobs? The Changing Structure of U.S. Wages*, Gary Burtless, ed. Washington, D.C.: The Brookings Institution.

Nielsen, Francois, and Arthur S. Alderson. 1997. "The Kuznets Curve and the Great U-Turn: Income Inequality in U.S. Counties, 1970 to 1990." *American Sociological Review* 62(1): 12–33.

Nord, Stephen. 1980a. "An Empirical Analysis of Income Inequality and City Size." *Southern Economic Journal* 40(6): 863–72.

Nord, Stephen. 1980b. "Income Inequality and City Size: An Examination of Alternative Hypotheses for Large and Small Cities." *Southern Economic Journal* 40(6): 863–72.

Nourse, Hugh O. 1968. *Regional Economics: A Study in the Economic Structure, Stability, and Growth of Regions*. New York: McGraw-Hill.

Novak, Michael, and Gordon Green. 1986. "Poverty Down, Inequality Up?" *The Public Interest* 83(Spring): 49–56.

Nozick, Robert. 1974. *Anarchy, State, and Utopia.* Oxford: Basil Blackwell.

O'Regan, Katherine and John Quigley. Summer 1996. "Teenage Employment and the Spatial Isolation of Minority and Poverty Households." *Journal of Human Resources* 31(3): 692–702.

Partridge, Mark D., Dan S. Rickman, and William Levernier. 1996. "Trends in U.S. Income Inequality: Evidence from a Panel of States." *Quarterly Review of Economics and Finance* 35(1): 17–37.

Persson, Torsten, and Guido Tabellini. 1994. "Is Inequality Harmful for Growth?" *American Economic Review* 84(3): 600–621.

Rawls, John. 1971. *A Theory of Justice.* Cambridge, MA: Harvard University Press.

Reich, Robert B. 1991. "Secession of the Successful." *New York Times Magazine* (January 20): 16–17, 42–45.

Roback, Jennifer. 1982. "Wages, Rents, and Quality of Life." *Journal of Political Economy* 90(6): 1257–1278.

Ryscavage, Paul, and Peter Henle. 1990. "Earnings Inequality Accelerates in the 1980's." *Monthly Labor Review* 113(12): 3–15.

Sawhill, Isabel V. 1988. "Poverty in the U.S.: Why Is It So Persistent?" *Journal of Economic Literature* 26(3): 1073–1119.

Sen, Amartya. 1973. *On Economic Inequality.* Oxford: Clarendon Press.

Shapiro, Robert Y., Kelly D. Patterson, and Judith Russell. 1987. "The Polls: Public Assistance." *Public Opinion Quarterly* 51: 120–130.

Slottje, Daniel J. 1989. *The Structure of Earnings and the Measurement of Income Inequality in the U.S.* New York: North-Holland.

Smeeding, Timothy. 1983. "The Size Distribution of Wage and Nonwage Compensation: Employer Cost vs. Employee Value." In *The Measurement of Labor Cost,* Jack Triplett, ed. Chicago: University of Chicago Press.

Sommers, Paul M. 1995. "Does Lower Income Inequality Improve a Country's Investment Climate?" *Atlantic Economic Journal* 23(4): 335.

Starobin, Paul. 1995. "The Politics of Anxiety." *The National Journal* 27(39): 2402.

Thurow, Lester. 1975. *Generating Inequality: Mechanisms of Distribution in the U.S. Economy.* New York: Basic Books.

Topel, Robert H. 1994. "Regional Labor Markets and the Determinants of Wage Inequality." *American Economic Review* 84(2): 17–22.

U.S. Bureau of the Census. 1982. *Census of Population and Housing, 1980. Summary Social, Economic and Housing Characteristics: United States.* Washington, D.C.: U.S. Government Printing Office.

_____. 1992. *Census of Population and Housing, 1990. Summary Social, Economic and Housing Characteristics: United States.* Washington, D.C.: U.S. Government Printing Office.

_____. 1991. *Statistical Abstract of the United States 1991*. 111th edition. Washington, D.C.

Wilson, William J. 1987. *The Truly Disadvantaged: The Inner City, The Underclass and Public Policy.* Chicago, IL: The University of Chicago Press.

Author Index

Headnote: *Italicized parenthetical numbers* following page locators refer to the number of citations for an author found on those pages. An italic *n* or *t* indicates a note or table, respectively.

Abramson, Alan J., 29, 179
Alderson, Arther S., 27, 32*n*8, 32*n*9, 183

Barro, Robert J., 27, 179
Bartik, Timothy, 20, 179
Benabou, Roland, 10, 30, 179
Blackburn, McKinley L., 22, 32*n*2, 179, 179*(2)*
Blank, Rebecca, 23, 97, 179
Blinder, Alan S., 32*n*1, 179
Bloom, David E., 22, 179*(2)*
Bluestone, Barry, 19, 179
Bobo, Lawrence, 15*n*6, 179
Boskin, Michael J., 143*n*1, 179
Bound, John, 19, 20, 179, 180*(2)*
Browne, Lynn E., 26, 180
Burtless, Gary A., 19, 22, 25, 26, 32*n*2, 180, 182

Card, David, 22*(2)*, 23, 97, 179, 180*(2)*
Carlino, Gerald A., 27, 180
Case, Anne, 30, 180
Cloutier, Norman R., 28, 88*n*2, 180
Crane, Jonathon, 30, 180
Cutler, David M., 5, 29, 31, 74, 88*n*5, 97, 141, 180*(2)*

Danziger, Sheldon, 26, 32*n*4, 32*n*7, 111*n*2, 181
Denton, Nancy, 29, 183
Dickie, Mark, 33*n*10, 180

Eberts, Randall W., 26, 180

Farber, Stephen C., 26–27, 181
Farbman, Michael, 32*n*4, 32*n*7, 181
Farley, Reynolds, 55*t*, 181

Fogarty, Michael S., 32*n*4, 32*n*7, 32*n*9, 181
Freeman, Richard B., 22*(3)*, 179*(2)*, 181*(2)*
Frey, William H., 55t, 181

Galster, George, 28, 32*n*8, 32*n*9, 88*n*2, 181
Garofalo, Gasper, 32*n*4, 32*n*7, 32*n*9, 181
Gerking, Shelby, 27, 33*n*10, 180, 181
Getis, Arthur, 5, 27, 181
Glaeser, Edward L., 5, 29, 31, 141, 180
Gopalan, S., 28, 32*n*8, 32*n*9, 88*n*2, 181
Gottschalk, Peter, 26, 32*n*2, 181
Green, Gordon, 74, 183

Harrison, Bennett, 19, 179
Haworth, Charles, 32*n*4, 32*n*6, 32*n*7, 181*(2)*, 183
Henle, Peter, 88*n*2*(3)*, 181*(2)*, 184
Holzer, Harry J., 30, 181

Ihlanfeldt, Keith R., 29, 30, 181

Jencks, Christopher, 30, 182
Johnson, George, 19, 20, 180*(2)*
Jorgenson, Dale W., 143*n*1, 179
Juhn, Chinhui, 20*(2)*, 25, 182*(3)*

Kain, John F., 29, 30, 182*(2)*
Karoly, Lynn A., 22, 25, 26, 27, 75*(2)*, 182*(3)*
Kasarda, John D., 29, 182
Katz, Lawrence, 19, 30, 74, 88*n*5, 95, 97, 180*(2)*, 182*(2)*
Klerman, Jacob Alex, 27, 182
Kosters, Marvin H., 32*n*2, 182*(2)*

Subject Index

Note: An italic *f*, *n*, or *t* following page numbers indicates a figure, note, or table, respectively.

190

196

About the Institute

The W.E. Upjohn Institute for Employment Research is a nonprofit research organization devoted to finding and promoting solutions to employment-related problems at the national, state, and local levels. It is an activity of the W.E. Upjohn Unemployment Trustee Corporation, which was established in 1932 to administer a fund set aside by the late Dr. W.E. Upjohn, founder of The Upjohn Company, to seek ways to counteract the loss of employment income during economic downturns.

The Institute is funded largely by income from the W.E. Upjohn Unemployment Trust, supplemented by outside grants, contracts, and sales of publications. Activities of the Institute comprise the following elements: 1) a research program conducted by a resident staff of professional social scientists; 2) a competitive grant program, which expands and complements the internal research program by providing financial support to researchers outside the Institute; 3) a publications program, which provides the major vehicle for disseminating the research of staff and grantees, as well as other selected works in the field; and 4) an Employment Management Services division, which manages most of the publicly funded employment and training programs in the local area.

The broad objectives of the Institute's research, grant, and publication programs are to 1) promote scholarship and experimentation on issues of public and private employment and unemployment policy, and 2) make knowledge and scholarship relevant and useful to policymakers in their pursuit of solutions to employment and unemployment problems.

Current areas of concentration for these programs include causes, consequences, and measures to alleviate unemployment; social insurance and income maintenance programs; compensation; workforce quality; work arrangements; family labor issues; labor-management relations; and regional economic development and local labor markets.